p i c a s s o

inside the image

PRINTS FROM THE LUDWIG MUSEUM · COLOGNE

EDITED BY JANIE COHEN

THAMES AND HUDSON

IN ASSOCIATION WITH ROBERT HULL FLEMING MUSEUM

IMPRINT

Published on occasion of the exhibition:
  PICASSO: INSIDE THE IMAGE · PRINTS FROM THE LUDWIG MUSEUM · COLOGNE

Robert Hull Fleming Museum · University of Vermont · March 4–June 4, 1995

First published in Great Britain in 1995
  by Thames and Hudson Ltd, London

First published in the United States of America in 1995
  by Thames and Hudson Inc., 500 Fifth Avenue, New York, New York 10110

ISBN 0-500-09251-6

British Library Cataloguing-in-Publication Data

A catalogue record for this book is available from the British Library

Library of Congress Catalog Card Number: 94-62008

Developed and produced by Verve Editions
  Gary Chassman · Julie Stillman

Designed by Robert A. Yerks

Printed and bound in Italy by New Interlitho

ACKNOWLEDGMENTS

Through the generosity of Peter and Irene Ludwig, the Robert Hull Fleming Museum has been given the extraordinary opportunity to organize an exhibition of graphic work by Pablo Picasso from the Ludwig Museum in Cologne, Germany. It is, thus, our privilege to bring a selection of Picasso's finest prints to the University of Vermont for the enjoyment of audiences in northern New England.

The Fleming Museum wishes to thank all who have contributed to the success of this project. We are especially grateful to Dr Evelyn Weiss, Deputy Director of the Ludwig Museum, Cologne, and to Dr Alfred Fischer, Curator of Prints and Drawings at that institution, for their help in organizing the exhibition. It would not have been possible without their generous and attentive assistance. We greatly appreciate the expert guidance of Gary Chassman and Julie Stillman of Verve Editions in producing this book, and the skill and dedication of Robert Yerks in creating its innovative design. Thanks are also due to Monica Rossi for her thoughtful translation of Dr Ludwig's interview, and to Katrin Velder for assistance in that effort.

The staff members of the Fleming Museum are owed a debt of gratitude in embracing this ambitious project, with special acknowledgment and thanks to Fleming Museum Registrar Christina Kelly and Exhibition Designer and Preparator Merlin Acomb. Curator and Assistant Director Janie Cohen's expertise in the late work of Picasso has been the guiding force behind this project; her achievements in creating the exhibition and book are most gratefully applauded.

Our deepest gratitude is owed to the Ludwig Foundation for Art and International Understanding and to Drs Peter and Irene Ludwig, whose support of the Fleming Museum and whose passion for Picasso have enabled us to study and enjoy the graphic works of the twentieth century's most exceptional artist.

Ann Porter · Director

The works in this exhibition, and consequently the prints reproduced in this book, are organized into thematic groups that focus on specific subjects Picasso explored in his printmaking over the course of his career. Some themes the artist returned to repeatedly over many years; others are associated with a particular period of his life. By organizing the work this way, we are able to see aspects of both evolution and continuity in Picasso's work in the graphic medium. Sections on **Technique** and **Style** highlight the range of Picasso's innovative printmaking techniques and his unorthodox, nonlinear approach to style, and also serve as an introduction to the thematic groupings. Examples are shown of lithography, linocut, etching, engraving, drypoint, aquatint, and mixed techniques, accompanied by five of Picasso's original print plates. **Portraiture** explores aspects of this genre in Picasso's prints, from straightforward portrayals to more esoteric examples in the artist's late prints, such as allegorical self-portraits and caricatured portraits of and after the old masters. **Mirada Fuerte/The Gaze** focuses on one of the most frequent themes in Picasso's work: the act of looking. This section includes prints from different periods that refer to the heightened visual sense at the core of Picasso's artistic life. **The Artist and His Model** is one of the most enduring themes in Picasso's oeuvre; this group includes works ranging from *The Sculptor's Studio* in *Vollard Suite* to the erotic encounters between artist and model in *Suite 347*. **The Minotaur and Classical Themes** features the masterpiece *Minotauromachy* and a selection of mythological and classical subjects from the *Vollard Suite* to the late prints. **Spanish Picaresque** looks at one aspect of Picasso's return to his Spanish roots at the end of his life, drawing from images of Celestina and related themes in *Suite 347* inspired by Fernando de Rojas's 1499 novel about an aging procuress. In **Variations After Rembrandt and Other Artists**, a selection of Picasso's prints from the 1930s through 1972 represent his extensive exploration of Rembrandt's work as well as his visual dialogues with Cranach, El Greco, Ingres, Manet, and Degas. Illustrations of Picasso's specific sources for the prints in the last section are found on pages 128 and 129.

While the works included in the exhibition represent aspects of Picasso's printmaking activity from 1904 through 1972, we have chosen to focus the texts on the artist's late prints, in recognition of the Ludwigs' early appreciation of this challenging period of Picasso's work. I am most grateful to the three distinguished individuals who have joined me in contributing their scholarship to this book: Professor Peter Ludwig, Aldo Crommelynck, and Professor Karen Kleinfelder.

Peter and Irene Ludwig have assembled one of the world's largest private art collections, housed today in museums in Aachen, Basel, Budapest, Cologne, Koblenz, Oberhausen, St Petersburg, and Vienna. Their diverse collections range from art of classical antiquity and pre-Columbian cultures to contemporary art from Eastern and Western Europe, North America, and Latin

America. In 1950 Peter Ludwig wrote his dissertation on Picasso, whose work engendered the Ludwigs' passion for art; Picasso is the only individual artist whose work they have collected in depth. In the interview published here, Professor Ludwig discusses the genesis of his interest in the artist and his views on various aspects of Picasso's work.

Master printer Aldo Crommelynck worked with Picasso for twenty years, first assisting him with his prints in Lacourière's workshop in Paris in 1949. Crommelynck set up a print workshop in Mougins in 1963 to accommodate Picasso's need for a printer close at hand. He worked closely with Picasso during the artist's final decade, becoming a part of his daily life and his creative process. Crommelynck was responsible for the printing of Picasso's final two print series, *Suite 347* and *Suite 156*, contributing his expertise on intaglio technique. Aldo Crommelynck remains an active printer working in Paris and New York. In a recent interview published here, he offers recollections and commentary on his collaboration with the most innovative graphic artist of the twentieth century. Sidebars of print techniques are provided for readers unfamiliar with the processes.

Art historian Karen Kleinfelder has staked out new territory within Picasso scholarship. In her 1993 book *The Artist, His Model, Her Image, His Gaze*, published by the University of Chicago Press, Kleinfelder examined aspects of Picasso's theme of the artist and his model from a variety of critical perspectives including the theoretical, textual, psychological, and philosophical. Professor Kleinfelder is on the art history faculty at California State University, Long Beach, and is currently investigating the relations between Picasso, Dora Maar, and Jacques Lacan. In the essay included in this book, she explores Picasso's late work in light of Lacan's theory of the gaze.

My own work on Picasso has focused on his unusual practice of exploring other artists' imagery in his own work: creating what is known in the musical world as "variations" on the work of old and modern masters. A specific interest of mine has been the exploration of Rembrandt's imagery in Picasso's work from 1967 to 1972 — the focus of an exhibition I curated at the Rembrandthuis Museum in Amsterdam in 1990. In the essay written for this book, I have turned my attention to the visual record in Picasso's late prints of his consideration of his own early work, his debt to the artistic legacy to which he felt himself heir, and his basic beliefs about the power and the limits of representation.

We offer these diverse perspectives on Picasso's late work in the belief that the complexity of the work warrants a multifaceted approach to its understanding, and in the hope that our enthusiasm might be shared by longtime Picasso fans and newcomers alike.

janie cohen

<small></small>

CURATOR AND ASSISTANT DIRECTOR

WHAT DO YOU CONSIDER PICASSO'S MOST SIGNIFICANT CONTRIBUTION TO TWENTIETH-CENTURY ART?

Pablo Picasso revolutionized form in the art of his time and consistently integrated it into an ongoing development that had evolved over centuries, even millenia. Picasso led European art to its highest peak in the twentieth century.

PETER LUDWIG

YOUR INTEREST IN PICASSO DATES BACK TO YOUR DOCTORAL THESIS ON THE ARTIST. WHAT WAS IT THAT INITIALLY SPARKED YOUR INTEREST IN HIS WORK?

When the Second World War ended with the capitulation of Germany, I was eighteen years old and had been a soldier for two years. I was on duty with the signal corps in Koblenz on the Rhine, the region where I am from, and was an invalid in a military hospital there for many months. Toward the end of the war I served in an army medical unit so that I could remain in the area. I witnessed the complete destruction of Koblenz by allied bombers. My mother died in the ruins of our home. After returning from a short imprisonment in one of the American prisoner of war camps in Kreuznach in late autumn of 1945, I began my studies, first in Bonn and subsequently in Mainz. In courses on art history, archeology, ancient history, and philosophy, I searched for answers to the questions: Where did we come from? Where are we going? The teachings of existential philosophy were very important to young people at that time, not only in Germany. We encountered reproductions of the works of Pablo Picasso for the first time. I was profoundly moved: the image of mankind that Picasso's art captured seemed true to life in an intensity that had never before been seen. For everything that was said of Picasso's art — it is dreadful, gruesome, and terrible — it seemed to me nothing other than a true reflection of reality. This is how I experienced people at that time and how I myself felt: dealt an inexplicable fate, full of anxiety and terror, defenseless and yet rebellious, always ready to survive, to begin again and not give up hope, filled with longing for understanding, for security, and for love.

"Picasso in Ourselves," a lecture by the German art historian Hermann Schnitzler, passionately influenced us as students.

I met my wife while I was studying at the university. She was two years younger than I, and just as impressed with the profundity and gravity of Picasso's art. My dissertation, "Picasso's Image of Man as an Expression of an Attitude to Life Conditioned by his Generation," argued that Picasso's art followed established views of the world and of life. These views were just as fascinating for his contemporaries, but the clarity of Picasso's representations remains unsurpassed.

THE EXTRAORDINARY BREADTH OF YOUR PICASSO COLLECTION HAS ALLOWED YOU TO FOLLOW THE DEVELOPMENT OF CERTAIN THEMES IN PICASSO'S ART. IN YOUR VIEW, HOW DID HIS APPROACH TO SUBJECT MATTER EVOLVE DURING THE COURSE OF HIS CAREER?

During his entire life Picasso's art was primarily devoted to the image of man. The comparatively few landscape representations and still lifes are also reflections of man. For Picasso it was never about the reproduction of outward appearance, but the conjuring of the interior, the soul of man. Portraits by the fifteen- and sixteen-year-old Picasso already attempt to depict the essence of the figures he painted. In Barcelona and in Paris the young artist reproduced the outcasts of society: the suffering and the downtrodden, the acrobats as symbols of the artist, and the poor. Picasso's themes portray the loneliness of man and call for understanding and sympathy. The themes did not change in the eight decades of his creativity.

PICASSO'S LATE WORK CAPTIVATED YOU AND YOUR WIFE IN A WAY THAT SURPASSED WHAT HAD MOVED YOU IN HIS EARLIER WORK. CAN YOU CHARACTERIZE WHY THE LATE WORK AFFECTED YOU SO STRONGLY, PARTICULARLY AT A TIME WHEN MANY PEOPLE REJECTED IT?

Picasso's late works commence in the beginning of the 1960s when the artist was over eighty years old. He was world famous, yet far more misunderstood than admired. For those opposed to modern art his name was synonymous with that which they rejected. Others admired him and his work. Materially, Picasso was wealthy and could afford anything. As he once said at this time, he wanted for nothing and he no longer had to impress anyone; neither for the judgment of others nor for the market. He felt completely free. And while holding on to the great theme of his life, the image of mankind, this freedom allowed him to begin anew. He had total mastery of all of the techniques. As a young boy he learned to paint and sketch from his father, an art teacher, before he could read or write. As a child prodigy, he graduated from the academy with distinction and was already held in esteem by experts. Picasso was brilliantly educated. The experience of being an active artist for decades allowed him in his old age to work intimately with form and color. This ease of execution thrilled and excited my wife and me upon our first encounter with these works.

PICASSO'S LATE WORK, PARTICULARLY THE PRINTS, ARE MARKED BY HIS INVOLVEMENT WITH THE IMAGERY OF THE OLD MASTERS. MANY THEORIES HAVE BEEN SUGGESTED AS TO WHY HE "CONFRONTED" HIS PREDECESSORS IN THIS WAY. WHAT IS YOUR INTERPRETATION OF PICASSO'S ENGAGEMENT WITH ARTISTS OF THE PAST?

Picasso, the greatest revolutionary of twentieth-century art, was at the same time a traditionalist. Picasso perceived himself to be one of a long line of leading European artists. The German Matthias Grünewald; the Spanish El Greco, Velázquez, and Goya; the Italian Titian; the Dutch Rembrandt; and the French Manet, Degas, Toulouse-Lautrec, and Cézanne are some of the masters who left their mark on Picasso's art. What they accomplished in their time Picasso wanted to further advance in his time. Picasso's relationship to the art of his Spanish homeland was especially close. In recognition of his ninetieth birthday, he was invited to temporarily hang some of his paintings at the Louvre in Paris, in an exception to the Museum's policy of not exhibiting the work of living artists. When asked

where he would like to show his paintings, he spontaneously answered: with the great Spanish painters, with Zubarán and the others. Picasso regarded himself as the culmination of the Spanish painters, and, as someone from the Mediterranean, he also explicitly included ancient culture. Recent research shows that one of Picasso's most famous paintings, the *Demoiselles d'Avignon*, was influenced less by African art (something that Picasso himself always said) than by an important composition of El Greco's that he was able to study in the collection of a Spanish friend in Paris. In his late works Picasso liked to depict himself as a Spanish musketeer of the seventeenth century, and in a few important self-portraits he wears a hat like that of Velázquez or Goya, which is again a typical sign of his admiration for artists of the past. It is also striking that Picasso, who was always clean shaven, has a beard in many paintings — this was an homage to his bearded father, to whom he owed so much, and who had first impressed upon him the works of the great masters of the past.

PICASSO'S LATE PRINT SERIES, *SUITE 347* AND *SUITE 156*, BOTH OF WHICH ARE IN YOUR COLLECTION, TAKE THE FORM OF A STREAM-OF-CONSCIOUSNESS NARRATIVE. HOW CAN WE BEST UNDERSTAND THEIR POSITION WITHIN PICASSO'S OEUVRE?

These last great graphic series are incredible, in the number of plates that Picasso completed for them alone. And he reworked the majority of these plates numerous times, since most of the prints seemed to him to need further work when they came out of the press. These series erupted from within him and tell stories of the corruptibility of love, of sexual violence and of human passion, of the tragedy of old age and of the longing for affection. In some images Picasso dreams of himself back in his youth with all of youth's power. Theater scenes appear in the prints; these entire series are like a world theater of our existence. Picasso refers to Degas as well, whose figure appears again and again in his images — another manifestation of Picasso as a traditionalist.

CUBISM FORESHADOWED THE ENORMOUS CHANGES IN EUROPE FOLLOWING WORLD WAR I. COULD YOU PLACE PICASSO'S LATE WORK IN THE SOCIAL CONTEXT OF ITS TIME?

Picasso's work mirrored his lifetime in an astonishing way. Yes, Cubism announced the enormous changes in society that took place in Europe after the First World War. Picasso's masterwork *Guernica*, created in 1937, became a prophetic expression of the European catastrophe in the Second World War. Picasso's later works show the dissolution of societal structures and the triumph of the individual, for whom society set almost no limits. All hierarchical order disappeared. Defenseless, without a message of salvation, and without integration within a protective infrastructure, man is alone with himself and his nature.

WHAT DROVE PICASSO'S FORMAL EXPERIMENTATION?

For decades, modern art meant an avant-garde that consistently conquered new fields of expressive possibility and for which the new was continually worth striving. Picasso, who as a painter, but especially as a sculptor, really cleared new territory and opened up the way for artists of his time, never strived for the new just for the sake of the new; his primary concern was with the eternal theme of man in his time. To achieve this representation of man, he applied new forms. To Picasso the formally new was of little importance; to him the constants in art were of supreme importance. This is seen in the fact that after a few years he abandoned the invention of the cubist forms that he had developed together with his friend Braque, in order to reaffirm the image of man once again in classical forms.

IF YOU HAD TO IDENTIFY ONE ASPECT OF PICASSO'S ART THAT DISTINGUISHES HIM WITHIN THE HISTORY OF ART, WHAT WOULD THAT BE?

Only a very few artists are granted the grace to be able to work for so long a period of time as Pablo Picasso. His productivity and his diligence cannot be admired enough. The work he left behind is absolutely unique in numbers alone. Picasso was nineteen years old as the twentieth century began and he was able to work for seventy-two years in this century. He gave expression to what occurred in the decades of this century. Everything that Europe did and that happened to it, what it advanced and what it destroyed, is found in Picasso's work. Few artists of his generation were not enthralled by the genius of this Spaniard, who drew them all into his sphere. Most measured themselves against him and he drove many to despair: the greatness of Picasso hung like a shadow over many other artists, taking away some of their light. Picasso and the artists of his time — a colossal topic.

WHAT HAS BEEN YOUR GUIDING PRINCIPLE IN COLLECTING PICASSO'S WORK OVER THE YEARS?

We began our Picasso collection in the 1950s. For four decades we have endeavored to allow Picasso, the man and the artist, to be evident in the works of our collection, which represents the course of his long life and his diverse forms of expression. Picasso the painter and the draftsman are just as painstakingly documented as Picasso the sculptor, the ceramist, and the master of prints. Picasso cannot be acclaimed highly enough, especially in his graphics. Only Rembrandt is comparable to him here. The technical refinement that Picasso commands in all spheres allows him an intensity and a profundity of expression that is literally fantastic. In addition to over 160 original works of paintings, sculpture, and pottery, we were able to acquire a great number of print plates from each of Picasso's creative periods, and several hundred prints. Our art collections in toto are enormous. They range from the art works of the ancient world, to the art of ancient America, to India, China, and Africa; from European antiquity through the many centuries to our present time. Only with Picasso have we consistently sought to represent an individual artist as a complete phenomenon. Picasso is, for us, a part of our own lives.

AACHEN, GERMANY · JULY 20, 1994

11

RECOLLECTIONS ON PRINTMAKIN

aldo crommelynck

WITH PICASSO

My association with Picasso began in the late 1940s when I was a student in the Paris print studio of Lacourière. Lacourière was a friend of my uncle's. I was introduced to him to learn about printmaking and I would go to the studio when I had time. After I had been there a few months, Picasso began showing up from time to time. He was familiar with the studio because Lacourière had been his printer before the war. As Lacourière grew older, he lost interest in the business and was there less and less. I knew more about printmaking than some of the artists who came to the studio to work, and I was faced with the situation of having to help them when Lacourière was not there.

Both original and reproductive prints were made in the studio. Lacourière had already made a number of reproductions of Picasso's work; Picasso would lend the work and Lacourière would copy it, like Jacques Villon had done. I recall that Lacourière was working on a reproduction of Picasso's gouache of a goat's skull. Things were not satisfactory to Picasso, because the reproduction was overworked. Picasso challenged me: he said to Lacourière, "give me the plate you made and Aldo will start anew, from the same image." Picasso destroyed Lacourière's reproduction; he used the image, but he completely changed it. I made another reproductive print, which took a long time. Picasso was pleased with it, and from that time on, I believe he trusted me. He asked me to work with him in his studio as well. He had all the necessary equipment, which he later moved to the south of France.

Picasso and I were working in his studio in Paris in 1955, when I was still at Lacourière's. We used to melt the sugar-lift for the aquatint process in the bathtub. It's a mess — the varnish used to cover the sugar on the plate is very sticky. Anyway, Picasso didn't mind the mess. He had made some plates, and he announced that we were not going to finish the plate we were working on because he had to go to the south of France. It was Friday, and he said he'd be back Tuesday. He never came back! After a while he phoned and asked me if I would buy everything he needed to make etchings in the south; his secretary and friend Jaime Sabartès would write a check for it. So I bought paper, plates, acid, and so on. But after a while I noticed that he wasn't making many etchings anymore. It was because he didn't have a printer nearby. So in 1963 I had the idea to set up a studio in Mougins to enable Picasso to make etchings again. My brother and I set it up, we didn't know if the plan would work.

It was a very small studio and I performed every function. In Paris I had printers when I needed to proof, but there I had to do everything myself, commuting between the print studio in the village of Mougins and Picasso's studio about a mile and a half outside of town. I would prepare the plates to proof which is inevitably a messy job: inking the plates and then cleaning them, then I'd deliver the proofs to Picasso and pick up new plates, returning to the studio to proof them — we often worked until after midnight. Even in his eighties Picasso still had a lot of energy. He would sleep late in the morning, have a late lunch and a late dinner, in the Spanish style. It was a lot of work, but I was always available, that was the condition. I would call from Paris from time to time to inquire when we might next do something together; he frequently took up my offer, but he would never summon me to the south of France on his own initiative. Sometimes we would arrange a date for me to deliver editions for him to sign. I would arrive in Mougins with just an overnight bag, and would end up staying for weeks, sometimes even months.

I think what attracted Picasso to the intaglio process was the variety of line quality that one can achieve: on the one hand, the ease with which the blunt needle moves through the etching ground, and, on the other hand, the resistance of the needle against the copperplate in the engraving process. For instance, when you use a blunt etching tool, if you don't press hard enough, you leave some of the waxy etching ground, which acts like a lubricant, preventing the acid from biting the plate. So sometimes Picasso pushed so hard, which was his manner even with drawing, that he would etch through the ground into the metal plate. You could remove the ground and not bite the plate—

Aquatint

Tiny particles of resin are distributed uniformly on the surface of the print plate to produce a continuous area of tone. Varnish is used to protect the surface either from the grains of resin or from the acid bath. Picasso used both liquid and stick varnish to create white forms against a black background.

it was like a drypoint. Even when the plate was bitten, sometimes you could feel the burr.

As Picasso's printer, I would suggest things to make the process simpler. The very first suggestion I made with regard to technique was in Lacourière's studio. Picasso was working on a woman's portrait, a rather large plate. I suggested he apply the acid directly with the brush — it was the first open-bite he made. In the late prints, he tried to do in one step what he had previously done in two or three stages. For instance, with a sugar-lift aquatint, you paint the sugar on a perfectly clean plate; when the sugar is dry, you cover the sugar with varnish, and when the varnish is dry, you dip the plate into water to dissolve the sugar. Where the sugar melts, the varnish lifts off. Finally, the plate is covered with a layer of finely grained resin and bitten in an acid bath. But frequently, Picasso would bite the resin-grained copperplate by hand, with a brush, so as not to have the same tone everywhere. Sometimes he'd change his mind and would start with a flat black base. Then to introduce variation in tone, he would rub his finger against his nose and then on the plate, to make the surface slightly greasy in places. The sugar wouldn't hold on a greasy surface, and the result would be a gray tone (#97 *Suite 347*, p 41). So he made several like that — very

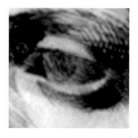

Drypoint

A sharp needle is pulled across the surface of the metal plate leaving a ridge of metal scrapings on either side of the incised line. Ink is caught in these ridges, called the burr, lending a velvety quality to the printed line.

efficient — it minimized the number of states and the use of equipment. He tried to do as much as possible in just one bite. Sometimes he would paint the sugar on the plate, then the hard ground, then lift the sugar; but then, before the resin ground was put on the plate, he would use a drypoint needle or scraper to make different kinds of marks on the plate, removing the ground in places (*#191 Suite 347*, p 64). Or sometimes he would remove the sugar with the sharp handle of the brush when it was still fresh, so as not to scratch the plate or disturb the varnish. Then after he had made marks with the scraper on the hard ground, I'd apply the resin. Then he would rework the plate with the scraper, removing both the resin ground and the hard ground.

The first marks made with the scraper would be black, because the hard ground was there. When you remove the hard ground and make a wide line, you remove everything, and the result is a gray line (*#40 Suite 347*, p 49). He knew how to achieve a variety of tones with one bite in the bath. If you know how he did it, you can see it in the prints. It creates a lot of texture. Another example: he would draw with a needle in the waxy etching ground. I provided him Q-tips and gasoline. He would remove the ground, but not completely — he didn't want that — just so it was greasy from the wax. Then he

bit the plate in the acid bath. The result was very strange, kind of like a fur coat (*#224 Suite 347*, p 106). The idea was also to make the process very simple.

Working with Picasso, there is no technical failure; it was the easiest thing to do. When he was dissatisfied with a plate, he would take it and scrape large areas, it didn't bother him. I offered to help, but he never accepted. It can be hard work, hours of scraping. He would use the marks of the scraper in a brilliant way, obtaining beautiful grays. He said, actually, that he thought each plate should be worked like that at the beginning, to achieve that nice quality! He was impressed by Rembrandt's print, *Ecce Homo*, which inspired a print of his own (*#10 Suite 156*, p 115). Rembrandt made drastic changes in *Ecce Homo*. In the first state he had a crowd, then the crowd disappeared and he added the arches in the foreground. I believe Picasso learned from that that you can make changes, even if it's difficult. If you change your mind, you can just rework the plate. From Rembrandt, he also learned that it was not necessary to make large prints in order to make good prints. Other artists also appeared in Picasso's late prints. He owned a group of

Etching

The surface of the print plate is covered with an acid-resistant coating that the artist scratches into with various tools to create the line. The plate is immersed in acid, which "bites" into those parts of the plate where the artist has scratched away the protective ground.

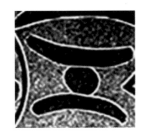

Linocut

Using a gouging instrument to cut away the linoleum, the artist removes everything from the block except for the areas to be printed. In later linocuts, instead of cutting a different block for each color, Picasso used the same block for the entire printing, resulting in the eventual destruction of the block.

Degas monotypes, *Maison Tellier*. He showed them to me and talked a lot about Degas as a human being as well as an artist. He appreciated how beautiful the monotypes were.

The way it worked in *Suite 347*, was that I provided Picasso with a stock of plates in various sizes, prepared with various grounds. I would identify the ground on the wrapping paper. The small plates were designed to illustrate a book, Fernando de Rojas's *La Célestine*, which we published in 1971. I would always write on the wrapping paper of the small plates, "Célestine." But the subject matter expanded onto the larger plates, which I couldn't use for the book. The theme influenced a large part of *Suite 347*; Célestine appears frequently. Making the book, *La Célestine*, was a difficult project. Picasso was extremely pleased with the size of the book and he suggested increasing the edition size. We were already printing a lot. But he thought they should be sold cheaply, like little loaves of bread at the market! When it came to his prints, however, Picasso was not at all interested in editioning them. He said one proof was enough. He was interested in the results that the medium could achieve — different lines, different surfaces — things he

couldn't do any other way. But one impression would be enough for him. When we had to edition to accommodate a dealer, Picasso was always most interested in seeing his recent work. When we editioned in 1968, for example, there were prints from 1963, '64, and '66 that were waiting for him; but he wanted to see the most recent ones.

It was a real pleasure to work with Picasso. It was known to the people around him that when he dedicated himself to printmaking, especially intaglio, he was in a good mood. The same was true with sculpture, he liked to make sculpture; he didn't mind seeing people, visitors. But when he was in a painting sequence, he didn't want to see anybody. Drawing on the etching plate was a very casual process for him. After the meal, lunch or dinner, but preferably late at night, he would take a small plate and work on it at the table, resting it against his knee. He would joke about many things, frequently about what he had just made. For example, it happened that a figure in one of his prints looked like someone we knew; but he hadn't done it on purpose — it's just how his memory worked. I noticed, on another occasion, that a character in something we were watching together on television appeared in his prints. Another time I was struck by the way he had drawn the entwined hands of a mother and daughter in one work. I asked

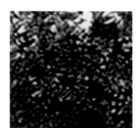

Sugar-lift Aquatint

The artist paints on the clean plate with a mixture of sugar and ink. The plate is then varnished and immersed in water whereupon the sugar melts and lifts off the varnish. The plate is then grained and bitten in those areas where the varnish has been stripped. When the plate is inked and printed, the areas that were painted in sugar print a rich black tone.

Lithograph

The image is drawn on limestone or zinc plate with a greasy crayon or a liquid called tusche. The stone or plate is then wet down with water. When printing ink is applied to the surface, it is repelled by the water and adheres only to the areas that have been drawn with the greasy medium.

him if he had drawn it from life. He said, no, not for that drawing, but that he had drawn so many hands over the years that he knew exactly where the fingers belonged. Even in the two late series of prints, when he distorted naked bodies so that the head was small and the legs and feet were large, the parts were always in the right place, it all worked together.

I don't know of any other artist who was as prolific as Picasso. Printmaking was quite natural for him. I believe that when he had an idea and made a drawing on the print plate, he was already thinking ahead to another possibility, which he made next. That's why there are so many plates. He would make series on the same subject matter, endlessly, but each one interesting and different. In my experience, Picasso was not the monster that many of his biographers portray. He was a pleasure to work with. I found him to be extremely easygoing, anytime, day or night.

Mixed Technique

Picasso frequently combined etching, drypoint, and aquatint techniques on the same plate as he reworked it through numerous states. He used a great variety of tools and introduced experimental materials such as grease into the aquatint process for special effects.

NEW YORK CITY

OCTOBER 17, 1994

FROM A CONVERSATION WITH JANIE COHEN

17

j...technique does its

ob, and you have only to busy yourself

with what

you're trying to find.

Pablo Picasso

TECHNIQUE

Portrait of Olga with a Fur Collar, 1923
Drypoint
19 ½ x 19 ⅜ in.

20

Bullfight, 1934
Copperplate
19 ½ x 27 ½ in.

23

Paloma and Her Doll on Black Background, 1952
Lithograph
27 x 21 ⅝ in.

24

Paloma and Her Doll on Black Background, 1952
Zinc plate
27 x 21 ⅝ in.

25

Large Head of a Woman with Hat, 1962
Linocut in four colors
25 ¼ x 20 ⅞ in.

Large Head of a Woman with Hat, 1962
Linoleum
25 ¼ x 20 ⅞ in.

Woman at the Window, 1952
Aquatint
32 ⅞ x 18 ¾ in.

Woman at the Window, 1952
Copperplate
32 ⅞ x 18 ¾ in.

29

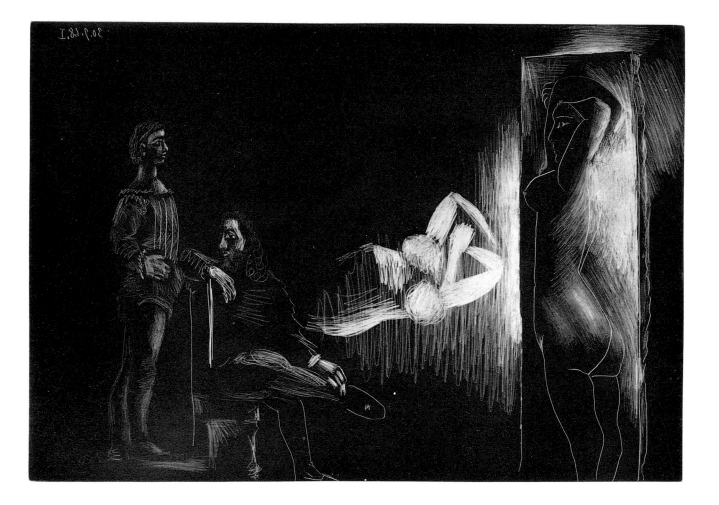

#344 *Suite 347*, 1968
Aquatint with solid varnish
8 ⅞ x 12 ¾ in.

#42 *Suite 347*, 1968
Aquatint with liquid varnish, drypoint
12 ⅜ x 15 ⅜ in.

#250 *Suite 347*, 1968
Sugar-lift aquatint, scraper
7 ⅞ x 12 ¾ in.

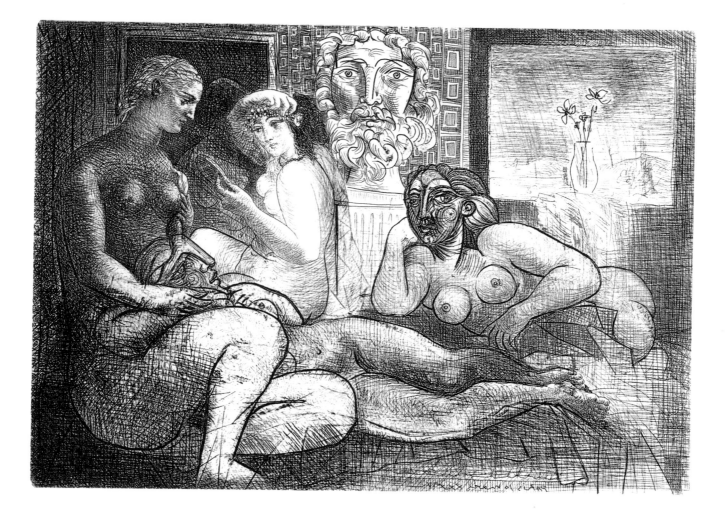

Four Nude Women and a Sculpted Head, 1934
#86 Vollard Suite
Etching, scraper, burin
8 ¾ x 12 ¼ in.

39

40

#34 *Suite 347*, 1968
Aquatint, etching
12 ⅜ x 15 ½ in.

#97 *Suite 347*, 1968
Etching, drypoint
13 ¼ x 19 ¾ in.

What is a face, really?

Its own photo?

Or make-up?

Or is it a face as painted by such or such painter?

That which is in front?

Behind?

Inside?

And the rest?

Doesn't everyone look at himself in his own particular way?

Pablo Picasso

Portrait of Vollard I, 1937
#98 Vollard Suite
Aquatint
13 ½ x 9 ⅝ in.

Portrait of Angela Rosengart, 1964
Lithograph
24 ⅜ x 18 ⅛ in.

#194 Suite 347, 1968
(Portrait after El Greco)
Etching
8 x 6 in.

47

#1 Suite 347, 1968
(Self-portrait and portrait of Jean Cocteau)
Etching
15 ½ x 22 ¼ in.

#101 Suite 156, 1971
(Portrait of Piero Crommelynck and family)
Aquatint
12 ⅝ x 16 ½ in.

48

#40 Suite 347, 1968
(Portraits of Picasso's mother, father, sister; Degas and Rembrandt)
Aquatint, etching, drypoint
8 ⅞ x 12 ⅝ in.

49

Exchanging Looks: Viewin

karen kleinfelder

PICASSO'S LATE GRAPHICS

There is a mysterious print from *Suite 347* (Figure 1, p 52) by the then eighty-seven year old Picasso that looks like the very end of vision. On the left, one of Picasso's musketeer figures enters the scene as nothing more than a sugar-lift aquatint blot and a scratchy patch of scraped lines; at center, facing forward with legs spread open is a seated female nude, her face and genital region blotted out despite her highly exposed position. On the far right, the blot, which had been circumspect or undercover in the aforementioned examples, now comes forward; a dark, shadowy form without contour, body, or figure, it registers as a stain, with all that might connote. This ambiguous blot makes for a kind of Rorschach moment, inviting us to read into it while at the same time defying a clear-cut reading. It is at the point of the blot, thus, that the viewer is drawn into the scene, precisely because this is the point where what is *seen* falls into question. Paradoxically, what seems to be a blind spot — the very end of vision — is the point where interpretation begins.

All of Picasso's late graphics contain such a point, though not always so blatantly. It is a question, then, of locating the blot, that point within the work that eludes our gaze and provokes it at the same time. My interpretation here is being guided in part by Jacques Lacan's psychoanalytic theory of the gaze: "In our relation to things, insofar as this relation is constituted by the way of vision, and ordered in the figures of representation, something slips, passes, is transmitted, from stage to stage, and is always to some degree eluded in it — that is what we call the gaze."[1] Peering closely at Picasso's puzzling image, one starts to get the uncanny[2] feeling that Lacan may be right: the picture has a gaze of its own,[3] which has the unsettling effect of throwing our gaze off center.

Looked at straightforwardly, the blot in the picture is nothing more than a stain, but in Lacan's eyes, it is the gaze itself that is *stained*. He, in fact, isolates "the function of *the stain*" as "that which governs the gaze most secretly and that which always escapes from ... that form of vision that is satisfied with itself in imagining itself as consciousness."[4] In other words, the stain is that dark underside of the gaze that eludes self-consciousness; hence, it undermines the reassuring self-possession of the Cartesian *cogito*, the subject who apprehends himself or herself as thought.[5] Lacan sometimes refers to the stain as having a scotomizing effect,[6] dimming vision or referring to a loss or obscuration of vision, like a shadow that cuts across the visual field, not unlike Picasso's blot. The stain also, thus, casts a shadow of suspicion, disrupting an otherwise idyllic scene. A dangerous supplement, the stain can take the form of a detail that does not belong or seems out of place.[7] What seemed ordinary enough takes an ominous turn as the stain that does not fit in — Picasso's blot — starts to suggest hidden meanings and dark secrets; suddenly things don't seem to be simply what they appear to be, and a straightforward gaze no longer will do.

Looked at askew, Picasso's blot sets into play a kind of *anamorphosis*,[8] one of those images distorted so that it can be viewed without distortion only from a special angle (the most famous example being Hans Holbein's *The Ambassadors* of 1533, in which a distorted skull is painted into the foreground of the scene, thereby throwing off what is seen otherwise — all those emblems of worldly power and knowledge that accompany the

Figure 1
#250 Suite 347
1968

ambassadors).[9] That is not to say that Picasso's blot ever truly falls into place or comes clearly into focus; viewed from whatever angle, it remains, in a very real sense, a blot that continually throws off our gaze.

The word "anamorphosis" stems from the late Greek *anamorphoun*, to transform, and certainly Picasso's blot

in this enigmatic image seems to form itself anew every time we try to pin it down: is it man or monster? orgasm or death? vision or virus? surplus or lack? A puzzle piece that won't quite fit, the blot "sticks out" here, like a phallic object.[10] A thicket of darkly stained jabbings, done with the end of the brush, the blot can also be "read" as a tangle of pubic hair, displaced from the nude at center, suggesting a castration anxiety magnified way out of proportion and looming up like a dark, menstrual cloud. It is little wonder that Brigitte Baer, who has devoted herself to the task of cataloguing Picasso's graphic output, found this image of the blot particularly difficult to decipher and categorize: "If the technique is fascinating, the subject is so mysterious that the onlooker can only guess at its meaning."[11] Despite the ambiguity of the mysterious blot, or perhaps precisely because of it, she felt compelled to title the image. What did the mysterious blot suggest to her? A "*Nightmare*."

The blot is truly a cataloguer's nightmare, frustrating any attempt to frame its form or fix its meaning. Perhaps what we need to do is to call a blot a blot, and let it stand as that, an ambiguous signifier that entices our gaze, but always manages to throw off our advances. The fact that we can neither master nor contain the image's possible meanings should not lessen our enjoyment. On the contrary, the highly suggestive blot, neither this nor definitively that, is precisely what opens the scene up to our gaze; black hole or not, it is our way in.

Once in, we find Picasso's late prints often seem more like "wet dreams" than "nightmares." Taken as a body, they are graphic graphics, indeed, the etchings of an eighty-year-old man. And the aged Picasso, highly self-conscious of his own mythology, shrewdly and ironically played on that image — the artist as a dirty old man. When *Suite 347* was first exhibited in Paris at Galerie Louise Leiris in 1968, the scenes of Raphael and his mistress, La Fornarina, were put on view in a private room and published separately as a supplement to the catalogue because the material was considered pornographic. Speaking about the censorship to a friend, Picasso voiced his objection, calling the series "quite innocent — I mean, quite natural. Well, you can imagine what they are about: Raphael and La Fornarina — his famous model — making love. Well, there's no need to exaggerate — it's not all sex. Raphael is painting in many of them, too."[12] I would agree; it's not all sex. The late graphics, including this explicit mini-series on the artist and model theme, are never simply about sex. They raise larger questions about creativity, the limits of representation, and the limitlessness of desire. The erotic is used as a double-fisted metaphor: art versus love, on the one hand, and painting as an act of love, on the other.[13] But then, if it's not all sex, it's not simply a matter of metaphor, either. Picasso's late graphics are *sexy*, and I don't mean to slight them as "Art" by saying that. On the contrary, consider what abstract painter Frank Stella had to say about Picasso, sex, and modern art: "Sex is no joke. When Picasso left the arid desert of Cubism behind, he never looked back. His women of the 1920s and 30s, awash in painterly volumetric rendering, left planar analysis with its future of modernist flatness standing on the beach. It is very hard for abstraction, or abstract figuration, to be sexy, and if it's not sexy, it's not art. Everyone knows that."[14]

In our current climate of censorship, I am not so sure everyone does know that, or would agree with that, but at least in this book several scenes from the erotic series have been openly included (pp 75, 76, 123). As for Picasso, he not only thought the images needed no censoring; he slyly suggested they be put to use as sex education manuals: "Instead of carrying on this foolishness [the censorship] with me, they'd be better off publishing a textbook for children with this catalogue. Don't you agree?"[15]

Picasso may have liked to make sex jokes *about* the late graphics, but sex is no joke *in* these prints. It is what opens up the theme of desire and all its discontents, from amorous longings to all-too-human fears of aging, impotence, and death.[16] "When I see a friend," Picasso confided, "my first impulse is to put my hand in my pocket to offer him a cigarette, as in olden days. But I know we don't smoke anymore. Even though age makes us give up certain things, the desire stays on. The same with love. We may not make it anymore, but the desire's there. I still reach into my pocket."[17] In the late graphics, the desire's there, all right, not only thematically but structurally in the very way the imagery plays itself out. Rather than unfolding sequentially according to "plotline," the late graphics as a group repeatedly frustrate the desire for narrative closure by sprawling beyond the boundaries. Various suites and series add up to an open-ended textual framework, in which Picasso places emphasis on the dynamics of the pictorial syntax more than any single component. The images do not simply build to a climax in which all desire is ultimately fulfilled and then closed off as everyone winds down to smoke a cigarette. If there is one thing that is made explicitly clear throughout the late graphics, it is that desire is never satisfied. Continually, it will both fall short of and override its goal, much like the act of representation itself, which can never completely close the distance between referent and image, but which often compensates for that lack with some kind of supplement, whether intended or not. The desired object, thus, can never fully account for the drive itself; according to the psychoanalytic model of desire derived from Freud and restated by Lacan, "desire is the desire for desire."[18] Continual deferral and the impossibility of closure are built into the very mechanism of desire, which is predicated on a psychic lack that cannot, by definition, be fulfilled. As Picasso himself summed up, "the desire stays on."

What seems, on the surface, at least, to drive the prolific output of Picasso's late graphics is the desired pursuit of the female nude (p 104), usually posed as the artist's model (*#166 Suite 347*, p 72) or as a beautiful, young maiden (sometimes a prostitute; p 126) who drives musketeers, circus performers, and old men to distraction. Always she is the object of the gaze (p 114), and though her body is put fully on display and nearly turned inside out by Picasso's "manhandling" of her form, she still seems to elude his grasp and total possession (p 73). "I paint . . . women. . . . Women, women, women. And yet can you say that it's Woman, just as she is? No. What I should like to do is to paint Woman as she is. . . . And that's what I've got to do."[19] Picasso sounds a bit desperate here, and with good reason. Woman "as she is" is no easy thing to define. When you go in search of an essence, what you inevitably end up with is none other than a blot, that ambiguous signifier that both overshoots its goal and comes up short. "I want to *say* a nude," Picasso told his friend, Hélène Parmelin. "I don't want to make a nude like a nude. I only want to *say* breast, *say* foot, *say* hand, belly. If I can find the way to *say* it, that's enough. I don't want

to paint the nude from head to foot, but just to be able to *say* it."[20] A look at the ever-proliferating chain of images that followed (only a selection of which are included here) suffice to show that what Picasso wanted to "*say*" quickly got lost in the "*saying*." When all is said and done, Picasso rather predictably reinforces the enigma of Woman more than he ever reveals her "essence." For him, Woman remains a highly cultivated mystery, and despite all his attempts to "*say*" otherwise, it is my belief that Picasso never truly wanted it any other way. Only by keeping her elusive could he carry on the pursuit; only as a constructed enigma — a blot, so to speak — could she provide him with the perfect pretext for playing out his own desire again and again.

The images end up telling us what Picasso could not, indeed, dared not "*say*." There is no equivalent — no model — for Woman, because she does not exist except as an imaginary construct (p 38). The very concept of Woman, with its insistent capital "W" and singular case, is predicated on the transcendent notions of a totality and a defining, universal essence. That no positive terms can in the end be isolated to sum her up definitively should not be taken negatively or as a lack in any real sense; there is something positive, after all, in the imaginary, idealized notion of Woman being demystified, even if that was not Picasso's stated agenda. While in pursuit of the Total Woman, he inadvertently created a more diverse and complex body of women's images than he is often given credit for (see p 39 for one such example). I say all this not in an attempt to redeem Picasso, known as the artist who "paints with his prick,"[21] but rather to point to that blot, once again, which defies all reductive categorization and disrupts too-easy stereotypes, even those leveled at Picasso (and perhaps supported by him through his own mythmaking tendencies). Picasso's desire to "*say a nude*" was from the first a desire to possess, control, and overpower Woman as the ultimate signified, but he can no more "*say*" the nude than can the many painters he pictures rather mockingly as they work away in vain before a nude model who forever eludes their grasp (*#58 Suite 156*, p 72). Picasso ends up "*saying*" something other than what he says he is saying, and therein lies the blot, which both spills over as an uncontrollable supplement and stops short of saying it all. It is precisely in that gap between surplus and lack that the blot once again opens up the possibilities for the play of meaning.

Figure 2
#191 Suite 347
1st state, 1968

Pursuit of the female nude seems, ultimately, to be more a pretext than the true force behind Picasso's prolific output in the late graphics; the obscure object of desire that drives the imagery turns out, instead, to be the gaze itself.[22] Artist David Hockney recognized as much; looking at Picasso's late work, he said: "It was the eyes that caught my eye and I realized it's about intense looking, what it does and what it can do."[23] We find ourselves, thus, back where we started, looking at our own looking. It is the gaze that seems to fill in all those gaps that open up between man and woman (*#196 Suite 347*, p 121), artist and model (*#45 Vollard Suite*, p 60), referent and image (*#64 Suite 347*, p 71), and it is our gaze, in turn, that Picasso will play on as he puts the act of looking on display again and again. At times, the gaze itself seems almost to "reach out and touch someone" (*#97 Vollard Suite*, p 112, and then again, thirty-five years later, in *#6 Suite 347*, p 62), as if that gap could indeed be closed. But if the gaze seems able to boldly go where no gesture ever could, a gap nonetheless remains open. Representation, it would seem, like desire itself, is predicated precisely on a gap or lack that can never, by definition, be completely filled. So the many artists Picasso pictures in these late graphics go on working, while we go on looking...

In the late graphics, Picasso does not just thematize the gaze; he acts out its intrigues. We see countless old men leering at beautiful, young women in every conceivable pose. Some look back, some simply look bored, but always the lure of the gaze is in full play, and on more levels than directly meets the eye, for our gaze is also scripted into the scene. We do not simply look on from a remove, like a voyeur who watches his subject from that privileged position of knowing that he is not watched in return. We instead see ourselves being seen by a gaze that eclipses our own. A case in point: in the first state of an aquatint print from *Suite 347*, made on the 26th of June, 1968 (Figure 2, p 55), we see a seventeenth-century Spanish cavalier ride into the scene on horseback; waiting as if to greet him, or lure him on, is a nude woman seated with legs spread apart and arms perched overhead in a pose that leaves little to the imagination. Centered in the background, as if to close the gap between man and woman, is the hooded form of an old procuress. With her haglike features, she makes quite a contrast to the beautiful, young nude at right. At this point, the narrative implications seem clear enough; it is as if we had stumbled into a scene from a picaresque novel, such as Fernando de Rojas's *La Celestina*, which Picasso knew well.[24] Watching the "courtship" unfold, the aged procuress seems to echo Celestina's lament: "Enjoy yourselves while you're young, for whoever gets a chance to do so but waits for a better one will regret it, just as I regret the few hours I wasted when I was a girl and had admirers and lovers. Now I am a decayed creature, withered and full of wrinkles, and nobody will look at me. Yet my mind is still the same: I want ability rather than desire. So kiss and make up and I'll enjoy watching you, which is the only pleasure I've got left."[25] Perhaps the aged Picasso could relate, identifying with the old procuress who sets the scene into action, but who then can only look on from the sidelines while the cavalier and young lady exchange glances, undoubtedly as a prelude for exchanging much more.[26] It's all in the look, but wait, the plot is about to thicken…

In the second state (Figure 3), Picasso makes some drypoint additions, and now what was covert and clan-

destine comes clearly out into the open: vector lines close the gap between man and woman as their gazes cross and lock onto their respective targets. But their gazes are not the only ones to get caught in the crossfire. The face of a bearded, old man now looks on from the background, one eye opened extra wide to take in the scene. While he casts a somewhat jealous look in the direction of the cavalier, the play of looks extends far beyond the pictured melodrama. With Picasso, it is never just what is pictured that counts; it is how something is pictured. And therein the plot thickens once again. Little does the cavalier know that as he ogles the

Figure 3
#191 Suite 347
2nd state, 1968

body of the young woman, he is being looked at in return, his gaze cut askew by the old man's evil eye. But he is not the only one who unsuspectingly becomes the object of another's gaze. When we turn to the old procuress, who we previously identified as Picasso's shadowy double, we find her look a bit more unsettling this time around. If vectors were drawn from her gaze outward, they would intersect the flirtation in the foreground, breaking through those lateral trajectories to extend directly outward in our direction. And it is here, while looking forward, that we see ourselves being looked at back.

Whose gaze, then, posits this scene as the transcendental subject who establishes point of view? Each perspective gets offset by another, and no single viewpoint, not even our own, gains sovereignty. One's eyes, it would seem, do not simply coincide with the gaze; a schism cuts through the visual field, and the subject is caught between the eye and the gaze.[27] The cavalier eyes the woman, but the cavalier is under the gaze of the old, bearded man in the background, and all this, of course, was subject to the gaze of Picasso himself,

which, though unseen, is alluded to (and eluded by) all that is seen. And what about us, the viewers, where do we fit into this picture? We both look on and are looked at; we are not all-seeing, and that, in fact, is what we come to see — our blind spots, or the limits on the horizon of vision itself. As Lacan says, "I see only from one point, but in my existence I am looked at from all sides."[28] This elision of the gaze leads to a "sliding away" of the subject,[29] or at least a radical decentering of the coordinates of the gaze. Picasso's late graphics not only show this, they act it out in an exchange of looks that underscores the slipperiness of both the gaze and the subject's position within a visual field that he or she can never completely master. The distinction between subject and object of the gaze becomes unclear when we, the viewers of Picasso's late graphics, become part of the scene. Both literally and figuratively, we are caught looking.

57

When the Andalusian fixes a thing with a stare, he grasps it.

his eyes are fingers holding and probing…

In Andalusia the eye is akin to a sexual organ…

David Gilmore

MIRADA FUERTE & THE GAZE

60

Sculptor and Kneeling Model, 1933
#45 Vollard Suite
Etching
14 ½ x 11 ⅝ in.

Boy and Sleeping Woman by Candlelight, 1934
#93 Vollard Suite
Etching, scraper, burin, aquatint
9 ¼ x 11 ⅝ in.

62

#6 Suite 347, 1968
Etching
16 ¾ x 13 ½ in.

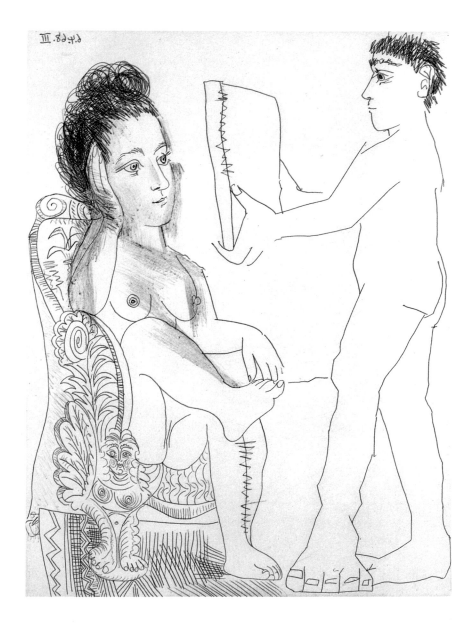

#19 Suite 347, 1968
Etching, drypoint
14 ¾ x 10 ¾ in.

#191 *Suite 347*, 1968
Aquatint, drypoint
6 x 8 in.

64

#25 *Suite 156*, 1970
Aquatint
8 ¼ x 5 ⅞ in.

If there were

only
one

truth,

you couldn't paint

a hundred canvases on the same theme.

Pablo Picasso

THE ARTIST & HIS MODEL

68

Sculptor and Model before a Bust, 1933
#15 Vollard Suite
Etching
10 ½ x 7 ⅝ in.

Sculptor and Model before a Window, 1933
#35 Vollard Suite
Etching
7 ⅝ x 10 ¼ in.

69

#39 *Suite 347*, 1968
Aquatint, etching
10 ¾ x 15 ⅛ in.

70

#64 Suite 347, 1968
Etching, drypoint
16 ⅜ x 19 ¼ in.

#58 *Suite 156*, 1971
Etching
8 ¼ x 5 ⅞ in.

72

#240 *Suite 347*, 1968
Aquatint, drypoint
7 ⅞ x 12 ¾ in.

73

#92 *Suite 156*, 1971
Etching, drypoint
8 ¼ x 5 ⅞ in.

#303 *Suite 347*, 1968
Etching
6 x 8 in.

75

#317 *Suite 347*, 1968
Etching
6 x 8 in.

#128 *Suite 347*, 1968
Aquatint, drypoint
2 ⅜ x 4 ¾ in.

#129 *Suite 347*, 1968
Aquatint, etching
2 ⅜ x 3 ⅜ in.

If **all the**

paths

I've taken were marked on a map and joined up with a line,

it might

represent

a minotaur.

Pablo Picasso

THE MINOTAUR & CLASSICAL THEMES

Drinking Minotaur, 1933
#59 Vollard Suite
Etching
11 ¾ x 14 ⅜ in.

Dying Minotaur, 1933
#65 Vollard Suite
Etching
7 ⅝ x 10 ½ in.

81

Minotaur Caressing a Sleeping Woman, 1933
#68 Vollard Suite
Drypoint
11 ⅝ x 14 ⅜ in.

Blind Minotaur Led by a Young Girl in the Night, 1934
#92 Vollard Suite
Aquatint, drypoint, burin
9 ¾ x 13 ⅝ in.

84

Minotauromachy, 1935
Etching, drypoint
19 ⅝ x 27 ¼ in.

Three Masked Figures and a Harpy, 1934

#94 Vollard Suite
Etching, aquatint
9 ¾ x 13 ⅝ in.

Winged Bull Watched by Four Children, 1934
#96 Vollard Suite
Etching
9 ⅜ x 11 ¾ in.

#35 Suite 347, 1968
Etching
12 ⅜ x 16 ⅜ in.

87

janie cohen

ENCOUNTER IN PICASSO'S LATE PRINTS

Picasso's final two print series, *Suite 347* (1968) and *Suite 156* (1970–72), contain a torrent of imagery expressed through a range of etching techniques unprecedented in the history of printmaking. Concerned solely with human encounters, the imagery contained in these prints has been described as Picasso's *"theatrum mundi"*[1]: the metal print plate provided the artist a stage upon which fantastical narratives were engraved, and, simultaneously, enacted. The players, as we will see, were drawn from Picasso's life, from his art, and from art history. Picasso was eighty-seven when he created *Suite 347*, and ninety-one when he completed *Suite 156*. It is not surprising that this visual diary reveals him to be examining his life: recalling his youth in Spain and his early influences, thinking about past loves, reassessing important points in the development of his work, comparing himself to the old masters in their late years, contemplating his place in history, dealing with aging and impotence, and, ultimately, confronting death. It is common wisdom that we all become "more like ourselves" in our old age; Picasso's late graphics reflect all that came before in his art, in an intensified form. The imagery that makes up his final two print series records the movement of Picasso's thought as he worked, day and night, in relative isolation, looking back upon almost ninety years of a compulsively creative life. The best way to appreciate fully the brilliance and complexity of these dreamlike images is to venture inside and meet the cast of characters. Toward that end, this essay will examine closely the imagery of one print from each of the two series. First, it will be helpful to identify some fundamental aspects of Picasso's creative process.

APPROPRIATION

One of the most provocative aspects of Picasso's work is the appropriation, exploration, and, ultimately, transformation of the work of other artists, which he carried out throughout his career.[2] Picasso's comments over the years indicate an active sense of rivalry with his artistic forebears and, at the same time, a profound sense of fraternity with them. Earlier in his career he had executed single paintings after works by artists before him; most renowned, however, are the long series of "variations" he made in the 1950s and 60s based on masterworks by Delacroix, Velázquez, and Manet.[3] In these lengthy cycles, Picasso deconstructed the composition, iconography, individual figures, style, color, and technique of the original work, until he reached an understanding of the artist's creative process that enabled him, in a very real sense, to possess the work himself.[4] With each confrontation, Picasso took greater liberties with the original work and pushed his exploration further, as if he were physically entering into the composition and stage directing it himself. His final sustained confrontation with an artist of the past was the most free-form of all: from 1966 until his death in 1973, he explored Rembrandt's paintings and etchings in countless of his own paintings, prints, and drawings[5] (pp 110–119).

Picasso's confrontations with other artists' work entered a new phase in the late prints, as memories of all of his previous "engagements" seemed to converge. *Suite 347* and *Suite 156* are filled with cameo appearances by escapees from the history of art, drawn from Picasso's phenomenal visual memory, who interact with one another and with figures from Picasso's past in scenarios never dreamed of by their creators (pp 110–127 and their sources on pp 128–129). The references in these etched fantasies are frequently humorous, irreverent, and erotic, as exemplified by an etching of May 10, 1968 (*#71 Suite 347*, p 114), in which Picasso animates Rembrandt's painting of the Danaë myth,[6] introducing Rembrandt's wife Saskia as a voyeur. Picasso shifts the viewer's perspective to the foot of Danaë's bed, while Cupid, who hangs precariously over Danaë's head as part of the bronze bed ornamentation in Rembrandt's painting, now swoops down on the figure, bow and arrow in hand. The narrative is further enriched by the fact that the nude voyeur is based on Rembrandt's 1633 silverpoint drawing of Saskia in a wide-brimmed hat, her head resting on her hand. This kind of quoting from the past takes place throughout Picasso's late print series. In addition to Rembrandt, there are references to Velázquez, Ingres, Manet, Degas, Van Gogh, and, as I shall discuss here, to Picasso's own early work and to the work of his earliest influences and Spanish compatriates, El Greco and Goya. The spirit in which these appropriations are carried out, as we shall see, shifts with Picasso's moods, from ribald humor to brooding introspection, to what might best be described as ritualistic invocation.

SIGN

Resemblance is achieved through an astounding economy of means in Picasso's late prints. Picasso said to his friend Brassaï in 1964: "An artist should observe nature but never confuse it with painting. It is only translatable into painting by signs. But such signs are not invented. To arrive at the sign, you have to concentrate hard on the resemblance."[7] *Suite 347* and *Suite 156* contain richly encoded imagery that culminates a lifetime's experience of inventing "signs" that capture the very essence of his subject. The process by which Picasso distills his subject — whether from nature or from someone else's art — can be described as caricature, albeit more profound in its identification of key characteristics and more subtle and complex in its depiction than most caricature. Caricature had played an important role in Picasso's work as early as his student days.[8] Through an adaptation of the representational strategy of caricature in his late prints, Picasso achieved the objective that he had expressed to friends several years earlier: "I want to *say* a nude. I don't want to make a nude like a nude. I want only to *say* breast, *say* foot, *say* hand, belly. If I can find the way to *say* it, that's enough. I don't want to paint the nude from head to foot, but just to be able to *say* it. That's what I want. When we're talking about it, a single word is enough."[9]

NARRATIVE

The prints in these two series possess a narrative quality unprecedented in Picasso's earlier work. Each print suggests an elaborate scenario involving enigmatic encounters between individuals or groups of figures; sequences of the prints suggest narratives, as well. Narrative had always been associated with the printmaking process for Picasso. In the *Vollard Suite*, created in the 1930s, for example, we see Picasso weaving a narrative through the Minotaur series, and the metamorphosis of imagery that occurs from one print state to the next also contains narrative elements.[10] That Picasso saw narratives in the changes between print states is further evidenced in several of the late prints in which his imagery incorporates the changes between states of several of Rembrandt's prints (pp 115, 118). In one case, Picasso creates an encounter between two figures that occupied the same position in different states of Rembrandt's *The Three Crosses*.[11]

Picasso was well-read[12] and was an accomplished writer himself.[13] Speaking to some visitors in 1968 about the prints from *Suite 347* inspired by Fernando de Rojas's *La Celestina* (pp 102–107), Picasso said "… As soon as the drawing gets underway, a story or an idea is born. … Then the story grows, like theater or life … I spend hour after hour while I draw, observing my creatures and thinking about the mad things they're up to. Basically, it's my way of writing fiction."[14] The narratives become increasingly complex when they incorporate aspects of Picasso's own past, and when they evolve through time and through several print states so that Picasso's actions on the print plate are directed by the memories and associations — from both art and life — that played through his mind as he worked. Memory, fantasy, conversation, books — literature and art books — and even television[15] provided the raw materials from which the images sprang as he chronicled the movement of his thoughts toward the end of his life. In 1935, Picasso made the statement: "I deal with painting as I deal with things, I paint a window just as I look out of a window. If an open window looks wrong in a picture, I draw the curtain and shut it, just as I would in my own room. In painting, as in life, you must act directly."[16] As Picasso's activities became increasingly

limited with advanced old age, his imagery recognized no limits. His art and life became one at last, as he created encounters on the metal print plates with the vitality and intensity with which he had lived his life.

Figure 1
Picasso, *#206 Suite 347*
1968

MAGIC

Much has been written about Picasso's conception of art as a form of magic.[17] Picasso's description of the revelation he had had early in his career regarding the role of art in African culture was recounted by his companion Françoise Gilot as follows: "Men had made those masks and other objects for a sacred purpose, a magic purpose, as a kind of mediation between themselves and the unknown hostile forces that surrounded them, in order to overcome their fear and horror by giving it a form and an image. At that moment I realized that this was what painting was all about. Painting isn't an aesthetic operation; it's a form of magic designed as a mediator between this strange, hostile world and us, a way of seizing the power by giving form to our terrors as well as our desires. When I came to that realization, I knew I had found my way."[18] Picasso referred to *Demoiselles d'Avignon* as his "first exorcism-painting,"[19] and he subsequently exorcised his fears, difficulties, and the deaths of friends through his painting. He was deeply superstitious and believed that through his art he could disarm evil forces and affect the course of events.[20] In the late prints, the forces that he confronted were his legacy and his death; we will observe him using his art to deal with both. Up until the very end, Picasso's art served a vital function in his life that had little to do with the formal concerns that characterized twentieth-century art in the Western world.

TWO NUDES REVISITED

Among the bawdy circus and brothel scenes that make up much of *Suite 347*, there are several images that suggest a more introspective mood. One of these, a dark, dramatic aquatint created on July 12, 1968 (Figure 1, p 91), provides an engaging point of entry into the workings of Picasso's mind and the imagery of the late prints. The scene unfolds in a dark room with a prison-like grate on the window. A nude woman in profile looks at two men in seventeenth-century attire who, in turn, gaze

Figure 2
Goya, *Time Will Tell*
ca 1814–20

upon two large nude women whose faces are turned away. The scenario that Picasso creates in this glowing aquatint is typical of the kind of enigmatic encounters that occur throughout his late prints. This image reveals the artist — now an old man — thinking back on a point in his life and his art when he stood on the threshold of radical discovery, and on the influences that shaped his development.

Picasso has borrowed both the prison-like setting and the stark, dramatic aquatint from the art of Francesco Goya, a fellow Spaniard and one of his earliest influences.[21] References to Goya's work appear frequently in the late prints as Picasso's thoughts drift back to Spain and to his early days as an artist.[22] Goya's ink and wash drawing *Time Will Tell* (Figure 2) provides the model for Picasso's dark interior[23] whose only sources of light are the grate-covered window, and, inexplicably, the women within.

Just as Picasso created new scenarios for figures from other artists' work, here he focuses on key players from his own art of sixty years earlier. The encounter that takes place within the room centers on a period in Picasso's work (1905–06) that is considered a watershed in the development of his art and in the history of modern art. The two nude women viewed from behind in the center of the composition suggest a curtain call by Picasso's *Two Nudes* of 1906 (Figure 3)—

the dramatic culmination of a year in which Picasso synthesized the influences of classical art, Iberian art, El Greco, Ingres, Gauguin, and Cézanne and embarked upon the cornerstone of modern art, the *Demoiselles d'Avignon*.[24] The bulky females who gesture mysteriously to one another in front of drapery in *Two Nudes* are transformed in the late print into an even more enigmatic pair, infused with the drama of another early Spanish influence, El Greco, and a work that may have been their original source.[25] Picasso seems to have had in mind here an

Figure 3
Picasso, *Two Nudes*
1906

unfinished, late work by El Greco, *Visitation* (Figure 4), which he may have seen in reproduction in 1906, but certainly knew in 1968.[26] In the late print, both heads are now turned away and the women's bodies are described with El Greco's dramatic lighting, created here by Picasso's aquatint brush.[27] The sense of mystery already present in *Two Nudes* is heightened in a way that reflects the expressionism of El Greco, Picasso's first real artistic "father figure," whose work had been a major influence on him in his formative years early in the century. In many of Picasso's variations after other artists, he presents what might have occurred between the protagonists just following the moment immortalized on canvas. Here he turns the game on himself: the woman on the left in *Two Nudes* has turned her head to follow the gaze of her companion into the darkness beyond.

The third woman in Picasso's print, the woman depicted in stark profile on the left side of the composition, further suggests that Picasso's thoughts had traveled back to his early work. Her thin stature, long wavy hair, sharp features, and hieratic profile evoke the women from Picasso's Rose period, immediately preceding the *Two Nudes*, such as *Woman with a Fan* (1905) (Figure 5, p 94), or the woman holding a mirror in *La Toilette* (1906). The *Woman with a Fan* has the same sharply defined nose and mouth, absence of expression, and light reflected on her face as the woman depicted in aquatint on the left of the *Suite 347* print. When one pictures her position on the right edge of the print plate on which Picasso worked, her resemblance to the long-haired, sharp-featured women staring blankly to the left in Picasso's work of 1905–06 is clear.[28] Details to which Picasso has given special emphasis in the late prints frequently indicate that he was referring to something specific. His very deliberate drawing of the woman's hair, for

instance, connects her again to his Rose period female figures that preceded the *Two Nudes*; in a series of paintings dating from 1906, Picasso depicted women dressing their own or another's long, wavy hair.[29] Another layer of reference can be found again in El Greco's *Visitation*; in a visual pun typical of Picasso, his tall, thin classical woman in black, white, and gray with columnar hair, echoes the fluted classical column in black, white, and gray at the left of the two women in

Figure 4
El Greco, *Visitation*
1607–1614

93

El Greco's painting. Visual associations and transformations such as this are a fundamental aspect of Picasso's art.

According to one of Picasso's closest friends in his late years, the artist often said that when he painted, he felt all of the great painters of the past and present standing behind him, watching.[30] The remaining players in this dramatic aquatint, the two figures on the right of the composition, are representatives of this pantheon of artists from the past that Picasso spoke of and depicted frequently in his later years. Rather than standing behind the easel observing the work in progress as he often portrays them (#64 *Suite 347*, p 71), here the two artists share the same plane of representation as Picasso's nudes and pass judgment on the women themselves. The artist on the left who points toward the women has the wide-brimmed hat and sharp features of Picasso's "Spanish" artists and cavaliers in the late prints; the figure on the right has the bulbous nose that is a frequent element in Picasso's caricatures of Rembrandt.[31] It has been suggested that Picasso's "dialogues" with artists from the past in his late years served as a substitute for the creative interactions with living artists and poets that had been so important in his earlier years.[32] Perhaps more relevant is the fact that his rivalries and relationships with the old masters, throughout his career, were

Figure 5
Picasso, *Woman with a Fan*
1905

as vivid and real to him as those he maintained with living artists. Comments he made through the years, as well as the nature of his variations after works by the old masters, attest to that. One can imagine Picasso joining in the conversation between the two seventeenth-century artists as they together look forward and back across the centuries, observing the influence earlier artists had on the birth of modern art. The image evokes a comment Picasso made to André Malraux in 1943: "What would Goya say if he saw *Guernica*? I wonder. I think he'd be rather pleased, don't you?"[33]

THEATER OF MEMORY

The prints of *Suite 156*, for the most part, contain even more layered imagery and complex meanings than those of *Suite 347*; in many of them the imagery evolved as Picasso reworked the plate through a number of states. #5 *Suite 156* (Figure 6), created in four states on January 25 and February 15, 1970, contains a cast of nine figures that come to the scene from the farthest corners of Picasso's past. Again we observe Picasso thinking back over his life, his art and its influences, and his role as progeny of the old masters. But this work takes us deeper into the web of Picasso's sources of inspiration, artistic processes, and belief systems. The focal point of the action in this print is a woman with raised arms, above whose head a large bird spreads its wings in flight. In the first state of the print her left hand holds the bird, in the third state Picasso adjusts her hand position, and in the final state she releases the bird. She is barebreasted and tilts her head backward to watch, her long, wavy hair flowing down her back. On the left half of the print, a group watches the action with fascination, while two figures on the right stare intently out at the viewer. A close reading of the figures in this print reveals the multiple levels of meaning with which Picasso endowed his images and illuminates the role that these prints played for him in animating the past.[34]

Picasso was deeply interested in the continuity of art forms from one culture to another, and, in his own appropriations of other artists' work, he was repeatedly drawn to works that were themselves based on earlier artistic forms or specific works of art.[35] The central figure in this image, the woman with upraised arms, vividly illustrates this aspect of Picasso's work. This figure has multiple sources in the work of Picasso's artistic precursors; sources that underscore his own acute awareness of his artistic legacy, particularly from the Mediterranean and Spain. Before looking at these, however, it is worth noting that Picasso may have again been thinking back to his own early work. A drawing of a mother with upraised arms dating from 1902 (Figure 7) — a study for an ambitious painting of a family deathbed scene conceived during a particularly difficult period in Picasso's early career and never executed[36] — suggests a visual memory, the subject of which, as we shall see, would resonate with the iconography of this print.[37] Turning now to the Mediterranean, the earliest source of inspiration for this figure is a late Minoan female idol (Figure 8, p 96) — a ceramic figure created on the island of Crete in the sixteenth century BC, with bare breasts and a skirt with a decorative

Figure 6
Picasso, *#5 Suite 156*
1970

Figure 7
Picasso, *Mother with Upraised Arms*
1902

pattern, upraised arms, almond-shaped eyes, snakes in her hands, and an animal on her head; other examples have birds atop their heads.[38] This figure represents a female deity and was found in the Palace of Minos at Knossos, a vast structure known in Greek legend as the labyrinth of the Minotaur.[39] In a typical Picassian leap through art history, he then followed the trail of this Mediterranean goddess to eighteenth-century Spain, where he found her reflection in the work of Goya. A drawing by Goya of Pasiphae (Figure 9, p 97), wife of Minos, King of Crete, who, in Greek mythology, seduced a bull and gave birth to the Minotaur, seems surely to have informed this image; her long, flowing hair and decorative dress are echoed in Picasso's print. Picasso had a deep knowledge of classical mythology, and Pasiphae's identity would certainly have attracted him. Goya's presence however, is most evident in the pairing of woman and bird. Here inspiration can be traced to several prints from Goya's *Caprichos*, a series of hallucinatory aquatints of human caprice published in 1799, the presence of which is felt throughout Picasso's late prints. In *Capricho #75*, (*Is there no one to untie us?*) (Figure 10), for example, a young woman bound at the waist to a man, raises her arms to fight off an enormous owl with outstretched wings.[40]

But the mix becomes richer yet, as we again observe forms from El Greco's art resonating in Picasso's memory.[41] El Greco's altarpieces and other religious paintings are filled with figures with upturned faces and arms reaching toward the heavens: St John, for instance, in El Greco's *Apocalyptic Vision* (Figure 11, p 98), who is similarly juxtaposed against a crowded composition of nudes. Owned at one time by a friend of Picasso's, this painting had a critical impact on Picasso's early work.[42] Perhaps of greater significance in El Greco's work is another source for the pairing of the woman and the bird in flight: the Virgin Mary and the Holy Spirit, depicted in works such as *Pentecost*, circa 1600, or the *Annunciation* (Figure 12, p 98). And, for Picasso, who delighted in combining various traditions, what could be a more natural union than ancient beliefs and Catholic dogma sharing one form?[43] Further, the association of the bird in flight with the Holy Spirit provides Picasso, the son, an entrée for the missing element of the Trinity, the Father.

The significance of the bird can be further explored in relation to the tall, bearded gentleman on the left

Figure 8
Late Minoan Female Idol
ca 1600 BC

edge of Picasso's print whose stare is fixed upon the outstretched wings: Don José Ruiz Blasco, Picasso's father, who appears in Picasso's earliest drawings and in his last prints.[44] Picasso's father was a failed painter whose subject of choice was the pigeons that he bred.[45] The seminal event of Picasso's early artistic development, when his father supposedly renounced painting and handed his brushes over to his son, occurred as a reaction to the skill with which the young boy had painted in the claws of a pigeon at his father's request.[46] The association between Don José and his pigeons remained strong in Picasso's mind throughout his life; in the 1950s, when Picasso's lithograph of a pigeon became world renowned as the *Dove of Peace*, he commented that he had "repaid him in pigeons."[47] Of equal import was the association in Picasso's memory between his real father and his earliest "artistic father," El Greco. Although Don José had encouraged his son to paint religious art,[48] he disapproved of Picasso's interest in El Greco's eccentric expressionism.[49] In addition, Picasso had remarked that El Greco's bearded men reminded him of his father in appearance.[50] In this theater of memory, antithetical forces converge into double identities. As Picasso once said, "In art, there is room for all possibilities."[51] Meanwhile, the two female nudes assuming artful poses in the fore- and background in this image refer to specific works of art. The nude in the doorway is Picasso's "sign" for Ingres's voluptuous, languishing nudes in *Le Bain Turc*, a painting that resonated in Picasso's work from 1905 to the end of his life. The elaborately etched, seated nude on a pedestal refers to Picasso's own sculpture, possibly to a similarly posed bronze nude on a square pedestal, dating from 1942.[52] The sculpture, which also watches the bird take flight, appears to be carried by a young man — the artist as a young man, who looks directly at the viewer. On the right side of the stage on which this drama is enacted, we find two figures who also look out of the image, with particularly intense gazes. Spaniards both, Picasso depicted them with the Andalusian trait for which he himself was renowned: *mirada fuerte* — the intense gaze.[53] The figure on the far right of the print is

Figure 9
Goya, *Pasiphae*
ca 1795

a reference to another Spanish painter who had occupied Picasso's attention earlier in his career, Velázquez. His appearance here is related to the first painting in Picasso's long series of variations after Velázquez's painting *Las Meninas*.[54] And finally, in the foremost figure on the right side of the print, the dwarf who stands to the immediate right of the woman, we find one of the most disturbing of Picasso's rare, late self-portraits. Picasso had represented himself as a dwarf, or an "old baby" in several prints in *Suite 347*.[55] This one, however, prefigures the chilling self-portrait of June 30, 1972 (Figure 13, p 99), in which Picasso looks directly at his impending death.[56]

Amidst all of this, absorbing it all, is Picasso represented as a dwarf — a figure who, according to Spanish belief, is endowed with magical powers[57] — his face reflecting fear of the future that he sees before him. But Picasso is yet elsewhere in this image. It is evident in his art, his life,[58] and his writing[59] that he identified with

birds; in a play written almost a quarter century earlier, Picasso represented himself as a bird-artist that sacrifices itself in order to acquire divine powers.[60]

It is also notable that throughout Picasso's career he created numerous images of women protectively holding birds – from *Woman with a Crow* (1905) to the *Blind Minotaur Led by a Young Girl in the Night* (1934) to examples in *Suite 347*,[61] they never let go until now. In the dark bird who takes flight above the woman in a double crucifix, Picasso finds the pigeon of his creation myth that embodied the transference of artistic power from father to son; the martyred artist; the holy spirit; the beginning and the end. Two years after this print was made we would see the bird come home to roost in the last known work of Picasso's life. In a stark,

Figure 10
Goya, *Is there no one to untie us?*
1799

scratchy pen drawing, a black bird looks directly into the open mouth of a man with the features of Picasso's father, surely one of the most haunting images of death in the history of art.[62]

Late in life, Picasso expressed his impatience with art historians who insisted upon one specific meaning for a given work; he believed the richness of an image was enhanced by its evocation of multiple meanings, including conflicting and incorrect ones.[63] Picasso perceived correspondences and symbolic significance all around him;

each component within his images is saturated with a multiplicity of meanings and referents. In the end, we are left with a complex, personal narrative that interweaves multifaceted references to Picasso's life and artistic influences, and, in the process, reveals some of Picasso's fundamental beliefs about the power of art.

The central figure with upraised arms who migrated through the centuries from ancient Crete to El Greco's to Goya's to Picasso's art, reflects Picasso's fascination with the "reincarnation" of images in art: in conversation with Daniel-Henry Kahnweiler in the 1950s, Picasso commented that there are basically very few subjects in art and that everyone repeats them; Venus and Cupid became the Virgin and Child and then Mother and Child, "but it's always the same subject."[64] Speaking with André Malraux several years before that, Picasso had discussed his belief in what he called "the Little Man from the Cyclades,"[65] the primordial artist who resurfaces throughout history in various cultures at various times. He had declared that "Painters are necessarily reincarnated as painters. They're a race in themselves," and had suggested that maybe he was "the Little Man."[66] In the same conversation Picasso wondered about the "necromancy" of artists,[67] the practice of conjuring the spirits of the dead in order to influence the course of events. He had used his art in this way before. In this image, it is as if Picasso were

Figure 11
El Greco, *Apocalyptic Vision*
1608–14

Figure 12
El Greco, *Annunciation*
1603–05

summoning all the power of his artistic forebears — his earlier incarnations — in order to exorcise his fear of death or, perhaps, to defy it, to secure his role as progeny of all artists who preceded him, and to reassure himself of the legacy that he was about to leave.

AND IN THE END

The perceptions about art that are revealed by Picasso's late prints reach back to prehistoric art, on the one hand, and, on the other, look to a future that emerged only after his death. He willed his art to serve a shamanistic role at the same time that he deliberately deconstructed artistic representation. He asked everything of his art and at the same time understood the profound limits of representation; as he had proclaimed as a young man, "... there are no concrete or abstract forms, but only forms which are more or less convincing lies."[68] Picasso's late work predicted the direction that art would take in the years following his death.

His understanding of the relativism of style, his strategies of deconstruction and appropriation, and the radical perceptions that prompted those explorations, all foresaw the conception of reality and representation that would prevail at the end of the twentieth century. Early in this century, Picasso had stepped outside of representation and had seen its shifting planes, perceiving the fact that there were many "more or less convincing lies." Throughout his life he remained true to that fundamentally postmodernist conviction.[69] Paradoxically, to the very end, he remained inexorably compelled by the drive to represent, to possess what he desired by capturing its visual essence, not by copying nature but by marshalling its power.

When Picasso was in his sixties, still a quarter century before he created the late prints, he said to Françoise Gilot: "I have less and less time, and yet I have more and more to say, and what I have to say is, increasingly, something about what goes on in the movement of my thought. I've reached the moment, you see, when the movement of my thought interests me more than the thought itself."[70] In his last years, age had opened the floodgates of memory and retrospection and, with his engraving tools, Picasso recorded it all. Once we learn the language and are able to read the texts, the late prints offer the opportunity to follow the movement of Picasso's thoughts through the labyrinth of memory — both personal and collective artistic memory — to the end.

Figure 13
Picasso, *Self-portrait* 1972

● ● ● ● as soon as the **drawing** gets underway,

a story or an idea is born…

Then the story grows,

like theater or life…   I spend hour after hour while I draw,

observing my creatures and thinking about the mad things

they're up to. Basically,

it's my way of **writing** fiction.

Pablo Picasso

SPANISH PICARESQUE

#87 *Suite 347*, 1968
Aquatint
11 ⅝ x 13 ½ in.

#221 *Suite 347*, 1968

Etching

12 ⅜ x 12 ⅜ in.

#105 *Suite 347*, 1968
Etching, drypoint
9 ¼ x 13 in.

#119 *Suite 347*, 1968
Aquatint
4 ¾ x 2 ⅜ in.

#134 *Suite 347*, 1968
Aquatint
13 ¼ x 19 ½ in.

Every painter takes himself for Rembrandt… everybody has the same delusions.

Pablo Picasso

VARIATIONS AFTER REMBRANDT

OTHER ARTISTS

Rembrandt and Women's Heads, 1934
#74 Vollard Suite
Etching
5 ½ x 8 ¼ in.

Rembrandt and Woman with a Veil, 1934
#81 Vollard Suite
Etching
11 x 7 ⅞ in.

111

Faun Uncovering a Sleeping Woman, 1936
(After Rembrandt: *Jupiter and Antiope*) #97 Vollard Suite
Aquatint, scraper, burin
12 ½ x 16 ½ in.

#66 *Suite 347*, 1968
(After Rembrandt: *Rembrandt and Saskia*)
Etching
5 x 3 ½ in.

113

*#71 **Suite** 347*, 1968
(After Rembrandt: *Danaë* and *Portrait of Saskia van Uylenburgh*)
Etching
12 ⅜ x 16 ½ in.

114

#10 Suite 156, 1970
(After Rembrandt: *Ecce Homo*)
Etching, aquatint, scraper
19 ¾ x 16 ½ in.

115

#19 Suite 156, 1970
(After Rembrandt: *Ecce Homo*)
Etching
12 ⅝ x 16 ½ in.

#15 *Suite 156*, 1970
(After Rembrandt: *The Nightwatch* and *The Artist Drawing from a Model*)
Etching, aquatint, drypoint, scraper
20 x 25 ½ in.

117

#24 Suite 156, 1970
(After Rembrandt: *The Three Crosses* and *Departure of the Shunamite Woman*)
Aquatint, scraper
5 ⅞ x 8 ¼ in.

#70 *Suite 156*, 1971

(After Rembrandt: *Rembrandt and Saskia* [*The Prodigal Son in the Tavern*])
Etching
8 ¼ x 5 ⅞ in.

119

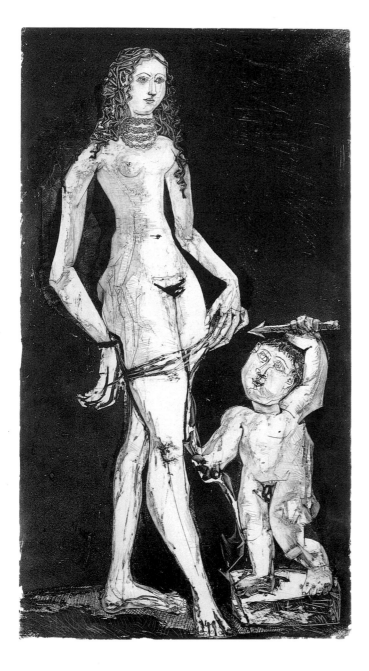

120

Venus and Cupid, 1949–51 (1979)
(After Cranach: *Venus and Cupid*)
Aquatint, etching, drypoint
31 ⅛ x 16 ⅞ in.

#300 *Suite 347*, 1968
(After Ingres: *Paolo and Francesca Surprised by Gianciotto*)
Etching
16 ⅜ x 19 ½ in.

123

#5 Suite 156, 1970
(After various sources, see pp 94–98)
Etching, scraper
9 x 13 in.

#29 *Suite 156*, 1970

(After Manet: *Déjeuner sur l'herbe*)
Etching
8 ⅝ x 11 in.

125

126

#16 Suite 156, 1970
(After Degas: *The Madam's Birthday*)
Etching
20 x 25 ¼ in.

#117 *Suite 156*, 1971

(After Degas: *The Madam's Birthday*)
Drypoint, scraper
14 ½ x 19 ¾ in.

#130 *Suite 156*, 1971

(After Degas: *The Madam's Birthday*)
Aquatint, drypoint, scraper
14 ½ x 19 ⅝ in.

127

SOURCES FOR VARIATION:

Rembrandt van Rijn
Jupiter and Antiope, 1659
(large plate)
Etching, drypoint, and burin

Rembrandt van Rijn
Rembrandt and Saskia, 1636
Etching

Rembrandt van Rijn
Danaë, ca 1636
Oil on canvas

Rembrandt van Rijn
The Artist Drawing from a Model, 1647
Etching, drypoint, and burin

Rembrandt van Rijn
The Nightwatch, 1642
(detail)
Oil on canvas

Rembrandt van Rijn
The Three Crosses, 1653
(2nd state, detail)
Drypoint, burin

Lucas Cranach the Elder
Venus and Cupid, 1530
Oil on panel

El Greco
The Burial of Count Orgaz, 1586
Oil on canvas

Jean-Auguste Dominique Ingres
Paolo and Francesca Surprised by Gianciotto, 1819
Oil on canvas

128

Rembrandt van Rijn
Portrait of Saskia van Uylenburgh, 1633
Silverpoint on parchment

Rembrandt van Rijn
Ecce Homo, 1655
(1st state)
Etching

Rembrandt van Rijn
Ecce Homo, 1655
(7th state)
Etching

Rembrandt van Rijn
The Three Crosses, 1653
(4th state, detail)
Drypoint, burin

Rembrandt van Rijn
Departure of the Shunamite Woman, 1640
Oil on panel

Rembrandt van Rijn
Rembrandt and Saskia, ca 1636
(*The Prodigal Son in the Tavern*)
Oil on canvas

Edouard Manet
Déjeuner sur l'herbe, 1863
Oil on canvas

Edgar Degas
The Madam's Birthday, 1878–1879
Monotype

129

1. Jacques Lacan, "Of the Gaze as *Objet Petit a*," in *The Four Fundamental Concepts of Psycho-Analysis*, ed. J-A. Miller, trans. A. Sheridan (1978; reprint, New York: W. W. Norton & Company, 1981), 73. The link between Picasso and Lacan is not merely a theoretical one. The psychoanalyst, who had a long term relationship with artists (he even published early on in the Surrealist periodical, *Le Minotaure*), was Picasso's personal physician for a time and the doctor who, at Picasso's request, treated the artist's mistress, Dora Maar, when she became severely depressed. I am currently investigating the relations between Picasso, Maar, and Lacan for a more extended study.

2. I use that word pointedly to make a covert reference to Freud's essay on "the uncanny" (see Sigmund Freud, "The 'Uncanny'," in *On Creativity and the Unconscious*, ed. B. Nelson [1919; reprint, New York: Harper & Row, 1958], 122–161). Playing on Schelling's notion that "everything is uncanny that ought to have remained hidden and secret, and yet comes to light" (130), Freud links the uncanny to repression: "the uncanny is nothing else than a hidden, familiar thing that has undergone repression and then emerged from it" (153). Freud cites several instances in which the uncanny is linked to the gaze: a fear of blindness or injury to the eye he sees as connected to castration anxiety; the dread of the evil eye; seeing one's double; and seeing something inanimate, like a picture, come to life. Lacan's idea of a picture having a gaze of its own (can a picture give you the evil eye?) also seems to fall under the heading of the uncanny, as does the stain or blot, the gaze's "repressed" underside. Slavoj Zizek plays on the notion of "the uncanny" very effectively when he uses Lacan's theory of the gaze to uncover what he calls "the Hitchcockian blot" (see Zizek, *Looking Awry: An Introduction to Jacques Lacan through Popular Culture* [Cambridge: The MIT Press, 1991], 88–106).

3. Lacan is hard to pin down on this point, as he is on so many others: "I shall advance the following thesis—certainly, in the picture, something of the gaze is always manifested.... The function of the picture—in relation to the person to whom the painter, literally, offers his picture to be seen—has a relation with the gaze. This relation is not, as it might at first seem, that of being a trap for the gaze. It might be thought that, like the actor, the painter wishes to be looked at. I do not think so. I think there is a relation with the gaze of the spectator, but that it is more complex" (101). Lacan's diagram (106), which remaps the gaze, the subject of representation, and the image-screen that intervenes, makes all-too-clear just how complex these relations are under Lacan's gaze: the spectator's position is no longer simply a unitary point that posits the scene for itself; as Lacan turns the perspective diagram back in on itself, the viewer's vantage point becomes a vanishing point belonging to a gaze that comes from without (see Norman Bryson, "The Gaze in the Expanded Field," in *Vision and Visuality*, ed. H. Foster [Seattle: Bay Press, 1988], 89–91, and Rosalind E. Krauss, *The Optical Unconscious* [Cambridge: The MIT Press, 1993], 183–84).

4. Lacan, 74.

5. Lacan, 75–85. For an explication and critique of Lacan's decentering of the subject by "the Gaze," see Bryson, 87–108.

6. Lacan, 83–84.

7. See Slavoj Zizek for a fascinating development of this "uncanny" turn of events in Lacan's theory; Zizek, 88–91.

8. In discussing the gaze, Lacan makes great use of the function of anamorphosis, "in so far as it is an exemplary structure" (85). Seeing a striking parallel in the contemporaneous development of geometral optics and the Cartesian subject, Lacan turns to anamorphosis to decenter the subject's position and to point to that repressed underside of the gaze. "This is why it is so important to acknowledge the inverted use of perspective in the structure of anamorphosis" (87).

9. Lacan uses the example of Holbein's *The Ambassadors* to show how "this strange, suspended, oblique object in the foreground" undercuts the scene by pointing to the *vanitas* (literally, emptiness) of the arts and sciences: "All this shows that at the very heart of the period in which the subject emerged and geometral optics was an object of research, Holbein makes visible for us here something that is simply the subject as annihilated" (88). For Lacan, the anamorphic function of the distorted skull is "*to catch in its trap*, the observer" (92). "This picture is simply what any picture is, a trap for the gaze. In any picture, it is precisely in seeking the gaze in each of its points that you will see it disappear" (89).

10. Lacan likens the distorted skull in Holbein's *The Ambassadors* to a "phallic symbol, the anamorphic ghost" (89), which points to an essential lack or castration anxiety. Like the stain or the blot, "this object, which from some angles appears to be flying through the air, at others to be tilted" (88) seems to stick out of place; "the secret of this picture is given at the moment when, moving slightly away, little by little, to the left, then turning around, we see what the magical floating object signifies. It reflects our own nothingness, in the figure of the death's head. It is a use, therefore, of the geometral dimension of vision in order to capture the subject" (92). Picasso's blot, an anamorphic ghost in its own right, likewise functions as a "trap for the gaze" (89).

11. Brigitte Baer, *Picasso the Printmaker: Graphics from the Marina Picasso Collection* (Dallas: Dallas Museum of Art, 1983), 182.

12. Picasso, in Robert Otero, *Forever Picasso: An Intimate Look at His Last Years*, trans. E. Kerrigan (New York: Harry N. Abrams, Inc., 1974), 178–79.

13. "Art is never chaste," Picasso said on more than one occasion (Picasso, in Dore Ashton, *Picasso on Art: A Selection of Views* [New York: The Viking Press, 1972], 15). Many writers have agreed with him, commenting on how Picasso explicitly connects the sexual act to the creative act in his art. See Robert Rosenblum, "Picasso and the Anatomy of Eroticism," 75–85, and Gert Schiff, "Picasso's *Suite 347*, or Painting as an Act of Love," 163–67, in *Picasso in Perspective*, ed. G. Schiff (Englewood Cliffs, NJ: Prentice-Hall, 1976). In a feminist critique, Lise Vogel voices a strong objection to Schiff's reading: "The approach is almost a caricature of the modern view that all creative work (Picasso's art, Schiff's interpretation, our appreciation) is essentially equivalent to sex from the standpoint of a man—with the ever-present implication that such endeavors are perhaps not quite so valuable, so virile, as a good fuck" (Vogel, "Fine Arts and Feminism: The Awakening Consciousness," in *Feminist Art Criticism: An Anthology*, ed. A. Raven, C. L. Langer, and J. Frueh [Ann Arbor: UMI Research Press, 1988], 29). Arguing for Picasso's sensitivity, on the other hand, is Marie-Laure Bernadac, who offers a compromise position by characterizing Picasso's late work as bisexual: "At the end of his life, the impending threat—and then the reality—of impotence led him to exploit to the full the resources of bisexuality ... bisexuality permits him, by exploring the female realm, to replace sexual potency with creative power" (Bernadac, "Picasso 1953–1972: Painting as Model," in *Late Picasso*, trans. D. Britt [London: The Tate Gallery, 1988], 89). Picasso's critics, it would seem, are more deeply divided than ever when it comes to the question of sexuality.

14. Frank Stella, *Working Space* (Cambridge: Harvard University Press, 1986), 76.

15. Picasso, in Otero, 179.

16. For more extended coverage of these issues, especially Picasso's fear and denial of death, see Karen L. Kleinfelder, *The Artist, His Model, Her Image, His Gaze: Picasso's Pursuit of the Model* (Chicago: The University of Chicago Press, 1993), chaps. 3, 4.

17. Picasso, quoted in Pierre Cabanne, *Pablo Picasso: His Life and Times*, trans. H. J. Salemson (New York: William Morrow and Company, 1977), 557.

NO

18. Lacan, quoted in Anika Lemaire, *Jacques Lacan*, trans. D. Macey (1977; reprint, London: Routledge & Kegan Paul, 1982), 164.

19. Picasso, In Hélène Parmelin, *Picasso says...*, trans. C. Trollope (London: George Allen and Unwin, Ltd, 1969), 114.

20. Ibid., 91.

21. Critiquing the ideology of the erotic at work in modern art, Carol Duncan targets Picasso's famous brothel scene, the *Demoiselles d'Avignon* (1907), as an example of how the image of the whore came to stand for the universal woman; building on this example, she adds: "The metaphor of the penis-as-paintbrush is a revered truth for many twentieth-century artists and art historians. It also insists that to create is to possess, to dominate, and to be quintessentially male" (Duncan, "The Aesthetics of Power in Modern Erotic Art," in *Feminist Art Criticism*, 62). Picasso's phallocentrism is widely criticized.

22. We find ourselves coming full circle here, back to Lacan's theory, which posits the gaze as the *"objet petit a,"* the object of desire that supports the scopic fantasy, as distinguished from the particularized gaze of another person. "In the scopic field, the gaze is outside, I am looked at, that is to say, I am a picture" (Lacan, 106). See Jonathan Scott Lee on "the gaze" in *Jacques Lacan* (Amherst: The University of Massachusetts Press, 1990), 154–61, and Krauss on Lacan, 87–88.

23. David Hockney, "Picasso: Or, the Important Paintings of the 1960s," in *David Hockney*, ed. A. C. Papadakis (London: Academy Press, 1988), 83. Hockney has always voiced high praise for Picasso's late work, even when it was not fashionable to do so. "The art world had viewed Picasso as though he'd died in around 1955, whereas he lived almost twenty years after that, and as far as I can see, did not decline at all: it's just harder to see what he was doing." Speaking broadly of the art of the 1960s, Hockney goes so far as to assert that "Picasso's is still by far the most inventive work done in that period and therefore the most important. If I suggest that the greatest painting of the 1960s was done in France by one man, I think any really serious look at it will back me up" (77).

24. According to John Richardson, who has access to the artist's personal library, Picasso owned several editions of Fernando de Rojas's *La Celestina*; see Richardson, "L'Epoque Jacqueline," in *Late Picasso* (London: The Tate Gallery, 1988), 29. See also Pierre Daix, "'Celestine' and Her Recurrence in the Work of Picasso," in Picasso, *La Célestine* (Paris: Éditions André Sauret, in association with La Galerie Didier Imbert Fine Art, 1988), 28–66.

25. *The Celestina*, trans. L. B. Simpson (1955; reprint, Berkeley: University of California Press, 1974), 108.

26. In his youthful blue period, Picasso painted Celestina with compassion, portraying her as an old, blind woman, but with dignity (Barcelona, 1903–04; see Christian Zervos, *Pablo Picasso*, vol. 1 [Paris: Editions Cahiers d'Art, 1932–1978], n 183). Now an old man himself, he depicts her, wrinkles and all, with the same degree of irony he uses on himself, or at least, that he uses on images of aging painters and shrunken old clowns. Like Celestina, the aged Picasso seems to have identified with the role of voyeur. "In front of your copper plate you are always the voyeur," he told Pierre Daix. "That is why I have engraved so many embracing couples" (Picasso, in Daix, 63).

27. "Must we not distinguish between the function of the eye and that of the gaze?" asks Lacan, who attempts to do just that in a lecture titled, "The Split Between the Eye and the Gaze." See Lacan, 67–78.

28. Ibid., 72.

29. Ibid., 75.

1. Gert Schiff, *Picasso: The Last Years, 1963–1973* (New York: Braziller, 1983), 11.

2. For an overview of this aspect of Picasso's work, see Klaus Gallwitz, *Picasso at 90, The Late Work* (New York: Putnam, 1971), 113–150; or Susan Galassi, "'Games of Wit': Picasso's Variations on the Old Masters," Ph.D. diss., New York University, 1991. A book by Galassi on the subject will be published by Abrams.

3. Picasso made 15 paintings, numerous drawings, and a suite of lithos after Delacroix's *Women of Algiers* (1954–55); 44 paintings after Velázquez's *Las Meninas* (1957); and 27 paintings, 140 drawings, 4 linocuts, and 12 cardboard maquettes after Manet's *Déjeuner sur l'herbe* (1959–1962).

4. See Timothy Anglin Burgard, "Picasso and Appropriation," *Art Bulletin* 73 (September 1991): 479–494, for a discussion of psychological aspects of Picasso's appropriation.

5. See Janie Cohen, "Picasso's Exploration of Rembrandt's Art: 1967–1972," *Arts Magazine* 58 (October 1983): 119–126; and *Picasso Rembrandt Picasso, Prints and drawings by Picasso inspired by works of Rembrandt* (Amsterdam: Museum het Rembrandthuis, 1990).

6. Picasso had done numerous variations on this Rembrandt painting, see Cohen, "Picasso's Exploration of Rembrandt's Art," 121, 126 (n 36).

7. Brassaï, *Picasso and Company*, trans. Francis Price (1964; reprint, New York: Doubleday, 1966), 162–163.

8. See Adam Gopnik, "High and Low: Caricature, Primitivism, and the Cubist Portrait," *Art Journal* 43 (Winter 1983): 371–376.

9. Hélène Parmelin, *Picasso says...*, trans. Christine Trollope (1966; reprint, New York: Barnes, 1969), 91.

10. See for example, the four states of *Four Nude Women and a Sculpted Head*, 1934, or the six states of *Faun Uncovering a Sleeping Woman*, 1936 (only the final state of each is reproduced here, pp 39, 112). Narrative elements were also evident in serial variations after other artists' work, and in individual works as well, such as *Guernica*, the *Minotauromachy* and *Blind Minotaur Led by a Young Girl*. One could speculate, in fact, that a narrative existed in Picasso's mind for most images he created.

11. See Cohen, "Picasso's Exploration of Rembrandt's Art," 123–24; *Picasso Rembrandt Picasso*, 60–71.

12. John Richardson notes that Picasso's library included "the Spanish classics ... most of French literature, English authors such as Swift and Stern, Americans such as Hawthorne and Melville, any number of thrillers, and of course art books of every kind..." (John Richardson, "L'Epoque Jacqueline," in *Late Picasso* [London: The Tate Gallery, 1988], 29).

13. Marie-Laure Bernadac, *Picasso: Collected Writings* (New York: Abbeville Press, 1989).

14. Roberto Otero, *Forever Picasso: An Intimate Look at his Last Years*, trans. Elaine Kerrigan (New York: Abrams, 1974), 170.

15. Richardson, "L'Epoque Jacqueline," 29.

16. Christian Zervos, "Conversation avec Picasso," *Cahiers d'Art* 10 (Paris, 1935), translation based on that of Myfanwy Evans in Alfred Barr, *Picasso: Fifty Years of His Art* (New York: The Museum of Modern Art, 1946), 273.

17. For the most comprehensive discussion of this topic, see Lydia Gasman, "Mystery, Magic and Love in Picasso, 1925–1938: Picasso and the Surrealist Poets," Ph.D. diss., Columbia University, 1981, (Ann Arbor: University Microfilms International, 1984), vol. 2.

18. Françoise Gilot and Carlton Lake, *Life with Picasso* (New York: Avon, 1964), 248.

19. André Malraux, *Picasso's Mask*, trans. June Guicharnaud with Jacques Guicharnaud (1974; reprint, New York: Holt Rinehart and Winston, 1976), 11.

20. Gasman, 538.

21. Picasso first copied one of Goya's *Caprichos* at the Prado in Madrid as a school boy in 1898, see Juan-Eduardo Cirlot, *Picasso: Birth of a Genius* (New York: Praeger, 1972), 66, 68, fig. 110.

22. The heavy presence of Spanish subjects and sources in Picasso's late work may reflect the return to one's beginnings often experienced at the end of life. In Picasso's case, the process was aided by the fact that among the few regular visitors he had at the end of his life were three Spanish friends, including a childhood friend, Manuel Pallarès. (Richardson, *A Life of Picasso* [New York: Random House, 1991], 1:102). Pierre Cabanne goes so far as to say: "Death and Spain: these were the old man's two constant obsessions." (Pierre Cabanne, *Pablo Picasso: His Life and Times*, trans. Harold J. Salemson [New York: Morrow, 1977], 8).

23. Brigitte Baer notes this source in "Seven Years of Printmaking: The Theatre and Its Limits," trans. David Britt, in *Late Picasso* (London: The Tate Gallery, 1988), 99.

24. Pierre Daix and Georges Boudaille discuss *Two Nudes* as the culminating painting in "the year of the great turning point." (*Picasso: The Blue and Rose Periods*, trans. Phoebe Pool [1966; reprint, Greenwich, Conn.: New York Graphic Society, 1967], chap. 5: 87–104.

25. This print is preceded in *Suite 347* by others that show Picasso's thoughts to have turned to Spain: scenes of Celestina and her *majas*, references to Goya (#201, July 5, 1968 II) and to El Greco in two prints just two weeks earlier (see pp 47, 121).

26. John Richardson notes that prior to 1906 Picasso "had access to a large repertory of El Greco reproductions" as his friend Miquel Utrillo was preparing a monograph on the artist, and that "Picasso had covered the walls of his studio with photographs of El Greco's work." (John Richardson, "Picasso's Apocalyptic Whorehouse," *New York Review of Books* 34 [April 23, 1987], 42). Richardson cites a number of Picasso's paintings of this period as having been influenced by El Greco, including *Boy Leading a Horse*, 1906; *The Blind Flower Seller*, 1906; and *Demoiselles d'Avignon*, 1907. Richardson notes a similarity between El Greco's *Visitation* and Picasso's *The Two Sisters* of 1902 (ibid., 42, and *A Life of Picasso*, 224), but to my eye the positions, gestures, contours, and drapery of El Greco's St Elizabeth and the Virgin Mary, as well as their sense of intimacy, would seem to have more directly informed Picasso's *Two Nudes*. If so, the *Visitation* had a similar impact on the development of *Two Nudes* as El Greco's *Apocalyptic Vision* (which is also a late work and is similar in style to the *Visitation*) had on the *Demoiselles d'Avignon*, and involves an analogous and typically Picassian conflation of the sacred and the profane.

27. The technique may also have been influenced by Degas's monotypes, see Brigitte Baer, *Pablo Picasso, Gli Ultimi Anni* (Rome: Accademia di Francia, 1987), 114.

28. See also the drawing for *Woman with a Fan*, 1905, reproduced in Richardson, *A Life of Picasso*, 1:423, and *Portrait of Madeleine*, 1904, a pastel and gouache drawing of a mistress of Picasso's, which came to light in 1968 when Picasso found it tucked into a frame, reproduced in Richardson, 302, and discussed in Pierre Daix, *Picasso Life and Art*, trans. Olivia Emmet (1987; reprint, New York: HarperCollins, 1993), 39. See also Daix and Boudaille, 278–82, for other profile portraits of this period.

29. See *La Toilette*, *Woman with Boy and Goat*, *The Harem*, *La Coiffure*, and *Woman Combing her Hair*, all of 1906. See Richardson, *A Life of Picasso*, 428, 445–447, regarding Picasso's interest in hair at this time. This figure also reflects Gauguin's Tahitian primitivism, which was an influence on Picasso in 1905 as well.

30. Parmelin, 40.

31. See, for example, #40 *Suite 347* (p 49).

32. Mary Mathews Gedo, *Picasso: Art as Autobiography* (Chicago: University of Chicago Press, 1980), 235, 258.

33. Malraux, 135.

34. My interpretation takes as its starting point observations about several of the figures made by Brigitte Baer in her discussion of the print in *Gli Ultimi Anni*, 162–3.

35. For instance, Manet's *Déjeuner sur l'herbe* or Rembrandt's *The Three Crosses*.

36. Richardson, *A Life of Picasso*, 254–55, 258. Richardson notes the figure raises her arms to heaven "in the manner of a seventeenth-century Niobe" — a figure from Greek mythology who implored the heavens after her children were killed by Apollo and Diana.

37. Picasso would again introduce this posture in the context of anguish in the right-hand figure in *Guernica*, which was based in part on Ruben's woman with upraised arms in *Horrors of War*, 1637–38.

38. See a late Minoan ceramic figure of a goddess with upraised arms and a bird on her head, from the Shrine of the Double Axes in Knossos (Spyridon Marinatos, *Crete and Mycenae* [New York: Abrams, 1960], fig. 132).

39. H. W. Janson, *History of Art* (New York: Abrams, 1986), 88.

40. This *Capricho* addresses the conflict between the Church's belief in the sanctity of marriage and the rationalist belief in the freedom of the individual. (José López-Rey, *Goya's Caprichos: Beauty, Reason & Caricature* [Princeton: Princeton University Press, 1953], 160–161). Picasso was never able to divorce his first wife, Olga, and this issue weighed heavily on him. See also *Capricho #20, Ya van desplumados (They are leaving, plucked)*, for source of the striations in the figure's hands and for the setting of Picasso's composition.

41. The fact that El Greco was born in Crete and achieved artistic prominence in Spain contributes another element of symmetry to the structure that Picasso has built.

42. Richardson, "Picasso's Apocalyptic Whorehouse," 46. Richardson notes that the painting "continued to reverberate in Picasso's work for the rest of his life."

43. For a discussion of Picasso's obsession with "the beliefs, imagery, superstitions, and spiritual power of the Church," see Richardson, 44.

44. See Beryl Barr-Sharrar, "Some Aspects of Early Autobiographical Imagery in Picasso's Suite 347," *Art Bulletin* 54 (December 1972): 516–533; and #40 *Suite 347* (p 49).

45. Each year Don José painted the pigeon of the year for Barcelona's Colombofila Society, of which he was president (Richardson, *A Life of Picasso*, 51). His masterpiece was a painting entitled *The Pigeon Loft*, painted in 1878, which was offered to Picasso as a gift on his 90th birthday by visiting officials from his birthplace and which he refused.

46. Richardson examines Picasso's "creation myth" and the fact that his father did continue to paint well into the twentieth century (ibid., 51).

47. Ibid., 52.

48. Ibid., 71.

49. Don José's response to his son's copying El Greco at the Prado in 1897 was "You're taking the wrong road." (Ibid., 95).

50. In a sketchbook sheet from 1898, Picasso combined a portrait of his father with caricatures of bearded men from El Greco's paintings, see Christian Zervos, *Pablo Picasso* (Paris: Cahiers d'Art, 1932–1978), 6:152.

51. Dore Ashton, *Picasso on Art: A Selection of Views* (New York: Viking, 1972), 121; reprint of Felipe Cossio Del Pomar, *Con las Buscadores del Camino* (Madrid: Ediciones Ulises, 1932), 118.

52. See Werner Spies, *Picasso: Das plastische Werk* (Berlin: Nationalgalerie, Stattliche Museen Preußischer Kulturbesitz, 1983), 278, #206.

53. David Gilmore, *Aggression and Community, Paradoxes of Andalusian Culture* (New Haven: Yale University Press, 1987). In his essay, "L'Epoque Jacqueline," *Late Picasso*, 30–31, John Richardson first cited Gilmore's explication of *mirada fuerte* in the context of Picasso. Picasso's gaze elicited such comments as "…his eyes were like laser beams in their intensity. They seemed to digest and devour everything they looked at." (William Rubin and Milton Esterow, "Visits with Picasso in Mougins," *Art News* 72 [Summer 1973], 48); or "When Picasso had looked at a drawing or print I was surprised that there was anything left on the paper, so absorbing was his gaze." (Leo Stein, *Appreciation: Painting, Poetry and Prose* [New York: Crown, 1947], 170).

54. The first state of this print follows closely Picasso's depiction of Velázquez's self-portrait in his August 17, 1957 painting. In the final state, as Brigitte Baer notes (*Gli Ultimi Anni*, 162), Picasso conflates it with his depiction of Philip IV reflected in the mirror of the same painting. Other references to *Las Meninas* and Picasso's variations on it are the figure within the doorway, the position within the composition and the facial expression of the dwarf, and the pigeon, which could be associated with the pigeons that accompanied Picasso during his work on *Las Meninas* (he had built a dovecote on the balcony outside the studio) and the paintings of them which Picasso considered part of the series and gave with the rest to the Museo Picasso in Barcelona.

55. See, for example, #8, March 25, 1968, or #82, May 13, 1968.

56. Pierre Daix recounts his conversation with Picasso about the 1972 self-portrait in Daix, *Picasso: Life and Art*, 369.

57. Rafael Alberti, *A Year of Picasso's Paintings: 1969* (New York: Abrams, 1971), 151.

58. Picasso grew up with his father's pigeons and as an adult kept birds himself — canaries, doves, pigeons, and owls (Gilot and Lake, 139).

59. See Gasman, 1235–1247, for discussion of bird symbolism in Picasso's art and writing.

60. *Les Quatres Petites Filles* was written in 1947–48 and published in 1968, see Gasman, 600.

61. #12, March 29, 1968, for example.

62. Reproduced in Baer, *Gli Ultimi Anni*, 351, #120.

63. Richardson, "Picasso's Apocalyptic Whorehouse," 44.

64. Ashton, 36; reprint of Daniel-Henry Kahnweiler, "Entretiens avec Picasso au sujet des 'Femmes d'Alger,'" *Aujourd'hui* 4 (September 1955): 12–13.

65. Malraux, 126.

66. Ibid., 143.

67. Ibid., 127.

68. Barr, 270; reprint of Marius de Zayas, "Picasso Speaks," *The Arts* 3 (May 1923): 315–326.

69. See Rosalind Krauss, "Re-Presenting Picasso," *Art in America* 68 (December 1980): 91–96, for a discussion of collage as "the opening of a rift with modernism" and the formative exercise in the "representation of representation," upon which Picasso's later historical paraphrasing was based.

70. Gilot and Lake, 118.

sources for quotations

Technique: Hélène Parmelin, *Picasso: The Artist and His Model, and Other Recent Works* (New York: Abrams, 1965), 114.

Style: André Verdet, *Picasso* (Geneva: Musée de l'Athenée, 1963); reprinted in Dore Ashton, *Picasso on Art: A Selection of Views* (New York: Viking, 1972), 96.

Portraiture: Anatole Jakovsky, "Midis avec Picasso," *Arts de France* 6 (Paris, 1946): 3–12.

Mirada Fuerte / The Gaze: David Gilmore, *Aggression and Community, Paradoxes of Andalusian Culture* (New Haven: Yale University Press, 1987), quoted in John Richardson, "L'Epoque Jacqueline," *Late Picasso* (London: The Tate Gallery, 1988), 31.

The Artist and His Model: Hélène Parmelin, *Picasso says…*, trans. Christine Trollope (1966; reprint, New York: Barnes, 1969), 115.

The Minotaur and Classical Themes: Dor de la Souchere, *Picasso in Antibes*, trans. W. J. Strachan (New York: Pantheon, 1960), 54.

Spanish Picaresque: Roberto Otero, *Forever Picasso: An Intimate Look at his Last Years*, trans. Elaine Kerrigan (New York: Abrams, 1974), 170.

Variations After Rembrandt and Other Artists: Françoise Gilot and Carlton Lake, *Life with Picasso* (New York: Avon, 1964), 45.

Endpapers: Michael Leiris, "The Artist and his Model," *Picasso in Retrospect*, ed. Sir Roland Penrose and Dr John Golding (New York: Harper & Row, 1973), 166.

References:

Bloch, Georges. *Pablo Picasso. Catalogue de l'oeuvre gravé et lithographié.* 4 vols. Berne: Kornfeld and Klipstein, 1968–79.

Geiser, Bernhard and Brigitte Baer. *Picasso, peintre-graveur.* Rev. ed. 5 vols. Berne: Éditions Kornfeld, 1986, 1988, 1989, 1990, 1992.

The Frugal Repast, 1904
Etching
46.3 x 37.7 cm · 18 ¼ x 14 ⅞ in.
Bloch 1; Geiser 2 II/a
ill. p 36

Nude in an Armchair, 1913/14
Etching
7.8 x 6.9 cm · 3 x 2 ¾ in.
Geiser 41
ill. p 37

Portrait of Olga with a Fur Collar, 1923
Drypoint
49.5 x 49.2 cm · 19 ½ x 19 ⅜ in.
Geiser 109 B
ill. p 20

Portrait of Olga with a Fur Collar, 1923
Zinc plate
49.5 x 49.2 cm · 19 ½ x 19 ⅜ in.
ill. p 21

Bullfight, 1934
Etching
49.5 x 69.7 cm · 19 ½ x 27 ½ in.
Bloch 1330; Geiser 433
ill. p 22

Bullfight, 1934
Copperplate
49.5 x 69.7 cm · 19 ½ x 27 ½ in.
ill. p 23

Minotauromachy, 1935
Etching, burin, scraper
49.8 x 69.3 cm · 19 ⅝ x 27 ¼ in.
Bloch 288; Baer 573 VII/B/c/1
ill. p 84

Vénus and Cupid, 1949–51 (1979)
Aquatint, burin, scraper, drypoint
79 x 43 cm · 31 ⅛ x 16 ⅞ in.
Bloch 1835; Baer 876 VI/B/a
ill. p 120

Paloma and Her Doll on Black Background, 1952
Lithograph
70 x 55 cm · 27 x 21 ⅝ in.
Bloch 727
ill. p 24

Paloma and Her Doll on Black Background, 1952
Zinc plate
70 x 55 cm · 27 x 21 ⅝ in.
ill. p 25

Woman at the Window, 1952
Aquatint
83.6 x 47.5 cm · 32 ⅞ x 18 ¾ in.
Bloch 695; Baer 891 II/A
ill. p 28

Woman at the Window, 1952
Copperplate
83.6 x 47.5 cm · 32 ⅞ x 18 ¾ in.
ill. p 29

Large Head of a Woman with Hat
February 9, 1962
Linocut in four colors
64 x 53.1 cm · 25 ¼ x 20 ⅞ in.
Bloch 1078; Baer 1293 IV/B/b
ill. p 26

Large Head of a Woman with Hat, 1962
Linoleum
64 x 53.1 cm · 25 ¼ x 20 ⅞ in.
ill. p 27

Portrait of Angela Rosengart, October 29, 1964
Lithograph
62 x 46 cm · 24 ⅜ x 18 ⅛ in.
Bloch 1843
ill. p 46

VOLLARD SUITE

Sculptor and Model before a Bust
#15 Vollard Suite, March 17, 1933
Etching
26.7 x 19.3 cm · 10 ½ x 7 ⅝ in.
Bloch 148; Geiser 300 B/d
ill. p 68

Sculptor and Model before a Window
#35 Vollard Suite, March 31, 1933
Etching
19.4 x 26.9 cm · 7 ⅝ x 10 ½ in.
Bloch 168; Geiser 321 II/B/d
ill. p 69

Sculptor and Kneeling Model
#45 Vollard Suite, April 8, 1933
Etching
36.7 x 29.7 cm · 14 ½ x 11 ⅝ in.
Bloch 178; Geiser 331 B/d
ill. p 60

Model and Surrealist Sculpture
#54 Vollard Suite, May 4, 1933
Etching
26.8 x 19.3 cm · 10 ½ x 7 ⅝ in.
Bloch 187; Geiser 346 B/d
ill. p 38

Drinking Minotaur
#59 Vollard Suite, May 18, 1933
Etching
29.7 x 36.6 cm · 11 ¾ x 14 ⅜ in.
Bloch 192; Geiser 351 III/B/d
ill. p 80

Dying Minotaur
#65 Vollard Suite, May 30, 1933
Etching
19.4 x 26.8 cm · 7 ⅝ x 10 ½ in.
Bloch 198; Geiser 366 B/d
ill. p 81

Minotaur Caressing a Sleeping Woman
#68 Vollard Suite, June 18, 1933
Drypoint
29.7 x 36.6 cm · 11 ⅝ x 14 ⅜ in.
Bloch 201; Geiser 369 II/B/d
ill. p 82

Rembrandt and Women's Heads
#74 Vollard Suite, January 27, 1934
Etching
13.9 x 20.9 cm · 5 ½ x 8 ¼ in.
Bloch 207; Geiser 405 B/d
ill. p 110

Rembrandt and Woman with a Veil
#81 Vollard Suite, January 31, 1934
Etching
27.8 x 19.9 cm · 11 x 7 ⅞ in.
Bloch 214; Geiser 413 B/d
ill. p 111

Seated Woman with Head Resting on Hand
#85 Vollard Suite, March 9, 1934
Etching
27.8 x 19.8 cm · 11 x 7 ¾ in.
Bloch 218; Geiser 423 B/d
ill. p 44

Four Nude Women and a Sculpted Head
#86 Vollard Suite, March 10, 1934
Etching, scraper, burin
22.2 x 31.3 cm · 8 ¾ x 12 ¼ in.
Bloch 219; Geiser 424 V/B/d
ill. p 39

Blind Minotaur Led by a Young Girl in the Night
#92 Vollard Suite, November, 1934
Aquatint, drypoint, burin
24.7 x 34.8 cm · 9 ¾ x 13 ⅝ in.
Bloch 225; Geiser 437 IV/B/d
ill. p 83

Boy and Sleeping Woman by Candlelight
#93 Vollard Suite, November 18, 1934
Etching, scraper, burin, aquatint
23.7 x 29.7 cm · 9 ¼ x 11 ⅝ in.
Bloch 226; Geiser 440 III/B/d
ill. p 61

Three Masked Figures and a Harpy
#94 Vollard Suite, November 19, 1934
Etching, aquatint
24.7 x 34.7 cm · 9 ¾ x 13 ⅝ in.
Bloch 227; Geiser 441 B/d
ill. p 85

Winged Bull Watched by Four Children
#96 Vollard Suite, December, 1934
Etching
23.7 x 29.8 · 9 ⅜ x 11 ¾ in.
Bloch 229; Geiser 444 B/d
ill. p 86

Faun Uncovering a Sleeping Woman
#97 Vollard Suite, June 12, 1936
Aquatint, scraper, burin
31.7 x 41.8 cm · 12 ½ x 16 ½ in.
Bloch 230; Baer 609 VI/B/d
ill. p 112

Portrait of Vollard I
#98 Vollard Suite, March 4, 1937
Aquatint
34.3 x 24.6 cm · 13 ½ x 9 ⅝ in.
Bloch 232; Baer 617 B/d
ill. p 45

SUITE 347

#1 Suite 347, March 16–22, 1968 I
Etching
39.5 x 56.5 cm · 15 ½ x 22 ¼ in.
Bloch 1481
ill. p 48

#6 Suite 347, March 24, 1968 II
Etching
42.5 x 34.5 cm · 16 ¾ x 13 ½ in.
Bloch 1486
ill. p 62

#19 Suite 347, April 6, 1968 III
Etching, drypoint
41.5 x 31.5 cm · 14 ¾ x 10 ¾ in.
Bloch 1499
ill. p 63

#31 Suite 347, April 12, 1968 I
Aquatint, etching, drypoint
32 x 47 cm · 12 ⅝ x 18 ½ in.
Bloch 1511
ill. p 33

#34 Suite 347, April 13, 1968 II
Aquatint, etching
31.5 x 39.5 cm · 12 ⅜ x 15 ½ in.
Bloch 1514
ill. p 40

#35 Suite 347, April 13, 1968 III
Etching
31.5 x 41.5 cm · 12 ⅜ x 16 ⅜ in.
Bloch 1515
ill. p 87

#39 Suite 347, April 15, 17, 1968 I/II
Aquatint, etching
27.5 x 38.5 cm · 10 ¾ x 15 ⅛ in.
Bloch 1519
ill. p 70

#40 Suite 347, April 15, 17–19, 1968 II
Aquatint, etching, drypoint
22.5 x 32 cm · 8 ⅞ x 12 ⅝ in.
Bloch 1520
ill. p 49

#42 Suite 347, April 19, 1968
Aquatint, drypoint
31.5 x 39 cm · 12 ⅜ x 15 ⅜ in.
Bloch 1522
ill. p 31

#64 Suite 347, May 5, 6, 7, 9, 1968
Etching, drypoint
41.5 x 49 cm · 16 ⅜ x 19 ¼ in.
Bloch 1544
ill. p 71

#66 Suite 347, May 6, 1968
Etching
12.5 x 9 cm · 5 x 3 ½ in.
Bloch 1546
ill. p 113

#71 Suite 347, May 10, 1968
Etching
31.5 x 42 cm · 12 ⅜ x 16 ½ in.
Bloch 1551
ill. p 114

#87 Suite 347, May 15, 1968 II
Aquatint
29.5 x 34.5 cm · 11 ⅝ x 13 ½ in.
Bloch 1567
ill. p 102

#97 Suite 347, May 16, 1968 VI
Etching, drypoint
33.5 x 50 cm · 13 ¼ x 19 ¾ in.
Bloch 1577
ill. p 41

#99 Suite 347, May 18, 1968 I
Aquatint
29.5 x 34.5 cm · 11 ⅝ x 13 ½ in.
Bloch 1579
ill. p 105

#105 Suite 347, May 23, 1968 I
Etching, drypoint
23.5 x 33 cm · 9 ¼ x 13 in.
Bloch 1585
ill. p 104

#119 Suite 347, May 27, 1968
Aquatint
12 x 6 cm · 4 ¾ x 2 ⅜ in.
Bloch 1599
ill. p 107

#128 Suite 347, May 30, 1968 I
Aquatint, drypoint
6 x 12 cm · 2 ⅜ x 4 ¾ in.
Bloch 1608
ill. p 77

#129 Suite 347, May 30, 1968 II
Aquatint, etching
6 x 8.5 cm · 2 ⅜ x 3 ⅜ in.
Bloch 1609
ill. p 77

#134 Suite 347, June 1, 1968 I
Aquatint
33.5 x 49.5 cm · 13 ¼ x 19 ½ in.
Bloch 1614
ill. p 107

#166 Suite 347, June 19, 1968 IV
Etching
12.5 x 9 cm · 5 x 3 ½ in.
Bloch 1647
ill. p 72

#191 Suite 347, June 26, 1968 IV
Aquatint, drypoint
15 x 20.5 cm · 6 x 8 in.
Bloch 1671
ill. p 64

#194 Suite 347, June 29, 1968 I
Etching
20.5 x 15 cm · 8 x 6 in.
Bloch 1674
ill. p 47

#196 Suite 347, June 30, 1968 I
Aquatint, etching
28 x 39 cm · 11 x 15 ⅜ in.
Bloch 1676
ill. p 121

#206 Suite 347, July 16, 18 I
Aquatint
31.5 x 39.5 cm · 12 ⅜ x 15 ½ in.
Bloch 1686
ill. p 122

#221 Suite 347, July 27, 1968 III
Etching
31.5 x 31.5 cm · 12 ⅜ x 12 ⅜ in.
Bloch 1701
ill. p 103

#224 Suite 347, July 29, 1968 I
Etching
15 x 22 cm · 6 x 8 ⅝ in.
Bloch 1704
ill. p 106

#240 Suite 347, August 4, 1968 I
Aquatint, drypoint
20 x 32.5 cm · 7 ⅞ x 12 ¾ in.
Bloch 1720
ill. p 73

#250 Suite 347, August 5, 1968 V
Aquatint, scraper
20 x 32.5 · 7 ⅞ x 12 ¾ in.
Bloch 1730
ill. p 32

#300 Suite 347, August 31, 1968 III
Etching
41.5 x 49.5 cm · 16 ⅜ x 19 ½ in.
Bloch 1780
ill. p 123

#303 Suite 347, September 1, 1968 III
Etching
15 x 20.5 cm · 6 x 8 in.
Bloch 1783
ill. p 75

#317 Suite 347, September 8, 1968 II
Etching
15 x 20.5 cm · 6 x 8 in.
Bloch 1797
ill. p 76

#344 Suite 347, September 30, 1968 I
Aquatint
22.5 x 32.5 cm · 8 ⅞ x 12 ¾ in.
Bloch 1824
ill. p 30

SUITE 156

#5 Suite 156, January 25, February 15, 1970
Etching, scraper
23 x 33 cm · 9 x 13 in.
Bloch 1860
ill. p 115

#10 Suite 156, February 3, March 5, 6, 1970
Etching, aquatint, scraper
50 x 42 cm · 19 ¾ x 16 ½ in.
Bloch 1865
ill. p 115

#15 Suite 156, February 16, March 2, 4, 1970
Etching, aquatint, drypoint, scraper
51 x 64 cm · 20 x 25 ½ in.
Bloch 1870
ill. p 117

#16 Suite 156, February 19, 1970
Etching
51 x 64 cm · 20 x 25 ¼ in.
Bloch 1871
ill. p 126

#19 Suite 156, March 11, 1970
Etching
32 x 42 cm · 12 ⅝ x 16 ½ in.
Bloch 1874
ill. p 116

#24 Suite 156, March 15, 16, 1970
Aquatint, scraper
15 x 21 cm · 5 ⅞ x 8 ¼ in.
Bloch 1879
ill. p 118

#25 Suite 156, April 1, 1970
Aquatint
21 x 15 cm · 8 ¼ x 5 ⅞ in.
Bloch 1880
ill. p 65

#29 Suite 156, April 9, 1970
Etching
22 x 28 cm · 8 ⅝ x 11 in.
Bloch 1884
ill. p 125

#58 Suite 156, February 25, 1971
Etching
21 x 15 cm · 8 ¼ x 5 ⅞ in.
Bloch 1913
ill. p 72

#70 Suite 156, March 8, 1971 II
Etching
21 x 15 cm · 8 ¼ x 5 ⅞ in.
Bloch 1925
ill. p 119

#92 Suite 156, March 25, 1971
Etching, drypoint
21 x 15 cm · 8 ¼ x 5 ⅞ in.
Bloch 1947
ill. p 74

#101 Suite 156, March 30, 31, April 1, 12, 1971
Aquatint
32 x 42 cm · 12 ⅝ x 16 ½ in.
Bloch 1956
ill. p 48

#117 Suite 156, May 1–4, 1971
Drypoint, scraper
37 x 50 cm · 14 ½ x 19 ¾ in.
Bloch 1972
ill. p 127

#130 Suite 156, May 19, 21, 23, 24, 26, 30, 31, June 2, 1971
Aquatint, drypoint, scraper
37 x 50 cm · 14 ½ x 19 ⅝ in.
Bloch 1985
ill. p 127

CREDITS

All of Picasso's work © 1995 Artists Rights Society (ARS),
New York/SPADEM, Paris. Photographs of works in Ludwig Museum,
Cologne courtesy Rheinisches Bildarchiv, Cologne.

Cohen essay

Pablo Picasso, *Two Nudes*, Paris (late 1906). Oil on canvas, 59 ½ x 36 ⅜ in. The
Museum of Modern Art, New York. Gift of G. David Thompson in
honor of Alfred H. Barr, Jr. Photograph © 1994 The Museum of Modern
Art, NY.

El Greco, *Visitation*, Dumbarton Oaks Research Library and Collections,
Washington, DC.

Pablo Picasso, *Woman with a Fan*. Gift of the W. Averell Harriman Foundation in
memory of Marie N. Harriman, © 1994 Board of Trustees, National
Gallery of Art, Washington.

Pablo Picasso, *Mother with Upraised Arms*, Musée Picasso, © photo R.M.N.

Francisco Goya, *Pasiphae (Girl and Bull)*, The Metropolitan Museum of Art,
Harris Brisbane Dick Fund, 1935 (35.103.7).

Francisco Goya, *Is there no one to untie us? (No Hay Quien Nos Desate?)*,
Los Caprichos, plate 75, The Metropolitan Museum of Art.
Gift of M. Knoedler and Co., 1918 (18.64[75]).

El Greco, *Apocalyptic Vision (The Vision of Saint John)*, The Metropolitan Museum of Art, Rogers Fund, 1956 (56.48).

Sources for Picasso's Variations

Rembrandt van Rijn, *Rembrandt and Saskia*, Harvey D. Parker Collection, courtesy of the Museum of Fine Arts, Boston.

Rembrandt van Rijn, *Ecce Homo (Christ Presented to the People)*, 1st
and 7th states, The Metropolitan Museum of Art, Gift of
Felix M. Warburg and his family, 1941 (41.1.34; 41.1.36).

Rembrandt van Rijn, *The Three Crosses (Christ Crucified Between the
Two Thieves)*, 2nd and 4th states, The Metropolitan Museum of Art, Gift of Felix M. Warburg and his family, 1941
(41.1.31; 41.1.33).

Rembrandt van Rijn, *The Nightwatch*, courtesy of the Rijksmuseum-
Stichting Amsterdam.

Rembrandt van Rijn, *Departure of the Shunamite Woman*, courtesy of
the Board of Trustees of the V & A.

Rembrandt van Rijn, *Rembrandt and Saskia (The Prodigal Son in the
Tavern)*, courtesy of Staatliche Kunstsammlungen Dresden.

Lucas Cranach, *Venus and Cupid*, Staatliche Museen zu Berlin —
Preußischer Kulturbesitz Gemäldegalerie.

Edouard Manet, *Déjeuner sur l'herbe*, Paris, Musée d'Orsay, © photo R.M.N.

Edgar Degas, *The Madam's Birthday*. Louvre, Photo © R.M.N.

Photographs of Picasso

David Douglas Duncan, *Picasso and Jacqueline*, p 76 (W. W. Norton, 1988), p 12.

David Douglas Duncan, *Picasso and Jacqueline*, p 54 (W. W. Norton, 1988), p 88.

From *Private Picasso* by Edward Quinn. Text and photographs © 1987 by Edward
Quinn; copyright © 1987 by Pierre Bordas et Fils, Paris and Ernst Klett-JG
Cotta'sche Buchhandlung Verlaggameinschaft; English translation © 1987
by Little, Brown and Co. By permission of Little, Brown and Co., p 50.

From *Picasso Photographe 1901–1916*, p 8.

David Douglas Duncan/Castellaras 53/MOUANS-SARTOUX 06370/France

VERVE EDITIONS
39 PINE HAVEN SHORES   SHELBURNE VERMONT 05482   TELEPHONE (802) 985-8671

(PS from below): Normally I never give permission for use of my shots. Too
complicated. However, curiously, at this moment a house guest is Miss Angela
Rosengart of Luzern, from whom Ludwig probably acquired many of the works in
your exhibit--as he also acqired many of his best "late" Picassos from her.
In any event, if you wish to use the shots and want to go to the trouble of

FAX 212-869-0856

shooting off the book, then I hope the photos will help you.

September 29, 1994

TO: Permissions Department
      W. W. Norton & Company
      500 Fifth Ave
      NY, NY 10110   Good luck with the catalogue--

FR: Julie Stillman

RE: Permission to reproduce two photos of David Douglas Duncan from
Picasso and Jacqueline

Dear Mr. Duncan,

I am writing to you on behalf of the Robert Hull Fleming Museum at the
University of Vermont. The museum is presenting a selection of Picasso's
late prints and print plates from the collection of Peter Ludwig at an
exhibition in the spring of 1995. For the museum exhibition catalogue we
would like to use two of your photos from *Picasso and Jacqueline*. The
photos are from page 54 ands page 76.

We would like to know if you will grant permission for their use and what
the fee would be to send us camera-ready material that can be
reproduced in the catalogue.

We are (of course) on a tight budget and schedule and I would like to hear
from you as soon as possible. I can be reached at 802-985-8671.

Thank you for your consideration.

Dear *Julie Still—*   16 October 1994

Your note via Norton was awaiting me upon return from the Frankfurt Book Fair.
Ludwig has some beautiful works of Picasso--and many others--so the Vermont show
should be a winner. No prints are available of the shots desired.